The Wholehearted Way

A Translation of Eihei Dōgen's *Bendōwa*
With Commentary by Kōshō Uchiyama Roshi

Translations by Shohaku Okumura
and Taigen Dan Leighton

Introduction by Shohaku Okumura

First published in 1997 by Tuttle Publishing, an imprint of Periplus Editions (HK) Ltd., with editorial offices at 153 Milk Street, Boston, Massachusetts 02109.

Library of Congress Catalog Card Number: 97-61460

DISTRIBUTED BY

USA
Charles E. Tuttle Co., Inc.
RR 1 Box 231-5
North Clarendon, VT 05759
Tel.: (800) 526-2778
Fax.: (800) FAX-TUTL

JAPAN
Tuttle Shokai Ltd.
1-21-13, Seki
Tama-ku, Kawasaki-shi
Kanagawa-ken 214, Japan
Tel.: (044) 833-0225
Fax.: (044) 822-0413

SOUTHEAST ASIA
Berkeley Books Pte. Ltd.
5 Little Road #08-01
Singapore 536983
Tel.: (65) 280-3320
Fax.: (65) 280-6290

First edition
05 04 03 02 01   00 99 98 97   1 3 5 7 9 10 8 6 4 2

Design by Frances Kay
Cover design by Christopher Kuntze

PRINTED IN THE UNITED STATES OF AMERICA

Dedicated to

Kanzan Hosokawa Yūhō Daiosho,
the late abbot of Sōsenji Temple
and founder of Kyoto Sōtō Zen Center

Contents

Foreword

*B*endōwa (Talk on wholehearted practice of the way) is one of the primary writings about practice/enlightenment by the great Japanese Zen Master Eihei Dōgen (1200–1253). After training as a monk in the dominant Japanese Tendai school and studying with the early Japanese Rinzai Zen teachers, Dōgen was dissatisfied with the Japanese Buddhist teachings of his time, and in 1223 went to study in China. After meeting his teacher and receiving dharma transmission, Dōgen returned to Japan in 1227. He eventually spread his teachings about Zen meditation and practice, and established a monastery to maintain this tradition. Dōgen is now honored as the founder of the Sōtō branch of Japanese Zen, which remains strong in Japan and in recent decades has spread in many places in the West.

Above and beyond any particular school of Buddhism or religious affiliation, Dōgen's profound and poetic writings are now generally respected as a pinnacle of Japanese philosophy and of world spiritual literature. Among Zen masters, Dōgen was a uniquely prolific writer. Especially renowned is his long masterwork, the collection of essays *Shōbōgenzō* (True dharma eye treasury), some versions of which include *Bendōwa*.

Bendōwa was written in 1231, soon after Dōgen's return from China to Japan. In this essay Dōgen expresses his teaching of the essential meaning of *zazen* (seated meditation) and its actual practice, elaborating on his brief initial writing, *Fukanzazengi* (The way of zazen recommended to everyone). Much of Dōgen's teaching encourages whole-hearted engagement in our lives, based on awakening to our intimate interconnectedness with the totality of our world and its creatures. Our intention in presenting this translation and commentary on *Bendōwa* is to make it available for the use and benefit of practitioners and sincere students interested in this profound, spiritual way of life recommended by Dōgen Zenji.

We have added notes to the end of the translation of the text to elucidate technical terms and Dōgen's references to the Buddhist and East Asian cultural traditions. Shōhaku Okumura Sensei's introduction provides valuable background on the place of *Bendōwa* in Dōgen's writings, as well as on some of the important developments in the Japanese Soto Zen tradition after Dōgen, of which very little has been available up to now in English. The introduction also discusses the essential meaning and etymology of "practice of the way" and of Dōgen's fundamental teaching of *jijuyu zan-mai*, the *samadhi* of self-fulfillment, which is elucidated in *Bendōwa*.

This book also features the lively and direct commentary of Kōshō Uchiyama Roshi, Okumura Sensei's teacher, who is one of the most highly respected modern Japanese Soto Zen masters. Some fine English translations from Dōgen's writings have appeared, and a few insightful scholarly treatments of Dōgen's teachings have been published in English; still, it is unusual to find a practical commentary like Uchiyama Roshi's, which expresses the down-to-earth implications of this subtle teaching for our everyday actualization. Uchiyama Roshi was successor to the great, dynamic Japanese master, Kodo Sawaki Roshi, who revitalized the practice of zazen in modern Japan before his death in 1965. From 1965 until his retirement in 1975, Uchiyama Roshi was abbot of Antaiji monastery, then in Kyoto, which was a primary place for Westerners to practice Zen in Japan during those years. He now lives with his wife in a small temple outside Kyoto and continues to practice the Japanese art of origami, of which he is also a master. Uchiyama Roshi has written many Zen texts and commentaries, some of which have been translated into English in *Refining Your Life* and *Opening the Hand of Thought*. We hope Western practitioners will savor this commentary on *Bendōwa*, selected from Uchiyama Roshi's talks to Zen students at Sōsenji Temple in Kyoto in 1978 and 1979.

In his introduction, Okumura Sensei describes his own long and devoted relationship to the *Bendōwa* text, which he first began translating over ten years ago. I was privileged to be able to collaborate in the final transformation of this text into English from 1990 to 1992, when it was used as a biweekly study class at the Kyoto Sōtō Zen Center at Shōrinji temple. The practitioners who visited Shōrinji to study and practice with Okumura Sensei during this time joined us in our challenging and detailed discussions of Dōgen's meaning and the difficulty of expressing it fully in English. These close investigations of the implications of English terms and their ramifications for Western practitioners were both stimulating and enriching.

Among those who contributed to the translation process through these discussions were Rev. Teijo Munnich, George Varvares, Laura Houser, Stephanie Simmons, Ann Overton, and Geula Rubin. Their help, based on sincere practice experience, greatly benefited this translation. Rev. Emyo Dielman also kindly assisted with the preliminary editing of our translation of Uchiyama Roshi's commentary.

I am personally very grateful to have had the opportunity to study Dōgen's teachings with Okumura Sensei. His sincerity and dedication, and his simple, everyday embodiment of wholehearted practice of the way, have been deeply inspiring.

An earlier version of some of Rev. Okumura's introduction appeared in *Zen Quarterly*, published by Sōtō Shū Shumuchō.

Taigen Leighton
Shōrinji

Introduction to Bendōwa

How the Bendōwa *was written and how it was transmitted.*

After spending five years in Zen monasteries in China and receiving dharma transmission from Tendo Nyojō Zenji, Dōgen Zenji returned to Kyoto, Japan, in the year 1227. He was twenty-eight years old. During the first few years after his return he stayed at Kenninji monastery where, from 1217 to 1223, he had practiced Zen with his late teacher Butsuju Myōzen (1184–1225) before they went to China together. Myōzen was one of the disciples of Eisai, the Japanese master who first introduced Zen to Japan and the founder of Kenninji. Dōgen's first writing, *Fukanzazengi* (The way of zazen recommended for everyone), was completed in 1227 right after his return from China.

But Kenninji was not the best place for him, as he wanted to transmit the buddha-dharma that he had received from Nyojō Zenji, and its style of practice is different from the Rinzai tradition. Also, as Dōgen mentioned in the *Tenzo Kyōkun* (Instructions for the head cook) and *Zuimonki* (Record of things heard), Kenninji monastery had lost the sincere spirit of practice established by Eisai. Dōgen left Kenninji in 1230, when he was thirty. Shōdō Nakaseko, a contemporary Sōtō priest and scholar, says in his *Dōgen Zenji Den Kenkyū* (Study on Dōgen Zenji's biography) that

1

Dōgen Zenji was forced to leave by the Buddhist establishment at Mount Hiei.

After Dōgen left Kenninji, he stayed in a small temple in Fukakusa, halfway between Kyoto and Uji, where Kōshōji is presently located. He did not yet plan to found his own monastery. These are the circumstances in which *Bendōwa* was written. In the second section of *Bendōwa* he said,

> I returned home in the first year of Sheting (1227). To spread this dharma and to free living beings became my vow. I felt as if a heavy burden had been placed on my shoulders. In spite of that, I set aside my vow to propagate this, in order to wait for conditions under which it could flourish. For now I will live alone, moving from place to place like a cloud or duckweed, and follow the way of the ancient sages.

Because students wanted to practice with him, he founded Kōshōji monastery in Fukakusa in 1233, when he was 33 years old. In the same year, he wrote *Genjōkōan* (Manifestation of reality) and *Makahannya Haramitsu* (Perfection of great wisdom), and he refined *Fukanzazengi*. The handwritten manuscript of the *Fukanzazengi* still exists and is called *Tenpukubon* (The version from the Tenpuku era).

In 1234 Koun Ejō joined Dōgen's *sangha* (community of practitioners) at Kōshōji and began to record the informal talks given by Dōgen Zenji that formed the *Shōbōgenzō Zuimonki*. Dōgen wrote *Gakudō Yojinshū* (Points to watch in studying the way) in the same year. *Tenzo Kyōkun* was written in 1237, and *Ikka Myōju* (One bright pearl) in 1238.

I think the writings of this period, that is from *Fukanzazengi* to *Ikka Myōju*, form one group of Dōgen's works. They were written in the early part of his teaching career, and they became the foundation for both the practice of his sangha and his later writings.

After 1238 he started to write many chapters of the *Shōbōgenzō* very rapidly. Before that I believe he did not write as much because he devoted himself primarily to creating his own monastery. After establishing his sangha, he wrote a number of chapters every year until 1246.

I have set out to translate those early writings of Dōgen Zenji that form the foundation of his teaching, that is, *Fukanzazengi, Bendōwa, Gakudō Yojinshū, Zuimonki, Tenzo Kyōkun, Makahannya Haramitsu, Genjōkōan,* and *Ikka Myōju.* Perhaps *Kyōjukaimon* [Comments on transmitting the precepts] should be considered among these early writings.

So far I have translated *Fukanzazengi* in the *Shikantaza* book, *Gakudō Yojinshū* in the *Dōgen Zen* book, and *Zuimonki.* I did a rough translation of the *Kyōjukaimon* for the last Tokubetsu sesshin at Daijōji. I worked on the translation of *Tenzo Kyōkun* with Daitsu Tom Wright when he did *Refining Your Life,* and have translated it with Taigen Leighton as part of our translation of *Eihei Shingi* (*Dōgen's Pure Standards for the Zen Community*), which begins with the *Tenzo Kyōkun.* The *Bendōwa* is presented in this volume.

I began to translate *Bendōwa* in about 1980, right after I came back to Japan from America. I had left Pioneer Valley Zendo in Massachusetts because of physical problems. My belongings were all in one backpack. I was completely broke. I had no job, and no place to live or practice. I was alone. I lived at a small nunnery called Seitaian in the north part of Kyoto city; it was owned by a friend who allowed me to stay as a caretaker. I lived and sat by myself except during five-day sesshins once a month. I supported myself by doing *takuhatsu* (monks' formal begging practice) a few times a month. In these circumstances, I was working on a translation of *Bendōwa.* Seitaian is near the former site of Antaiji. It is near the memorial monument to Kōdō Sawaki Roshi. Since I was in such a similar situation and I was 32 years old, the same age as Dōgen Zenji when he wrote *Bendōwa,* I felt that I really understood Dōgen Zenji's vow and motivation for writing *Bendōwa.* I was living a way of life similar to Dōgen Zenji's life in Fukakusa.

In the ten years after writing *Bendōwa*, Dōgen produced many other writings, but ten years after starting this translation, I am still working on *Bendōwa*. I have given up trying to compete with Dōgen Zenji.

Bendōwa was written in Fukakusa when Dōgen Zenji was staying there alone. Since he did not have his own monastery, not many people could visit him to ask about the dharma. He wanted to leave what he had learned from his teacher in China for sincere practitioners who were looking for the true dharma. He said in the *Bendōwa*:

> There might be some sincere practitioners who on their own do not seek after fame or profit and who give priority to the mind that seeks the Way. But they still may be vainly led astray by false teachers, and recklessly cover up correct understanding and become drunk in their own confusion, sinking into delusion for a long time. How will it be possible for them to nurture the true seed of *prajna* (ultimate wisdom) and have appropriate occasion to attain the Way? Since this unworthy wayfarer [Dōgen] is now living like a cloud or duckweed, how will they find the mountain or river where they can visit me? Because I care about these people, I have recollected and written about what I saw with my own eyes of the style of practice in the Zen monasteries of Song China, and what I received and uphold as the profound teaching of my master. I leave this for devoted practitioners of the way of serenity in order to let them know about the true dharma of buddhas.

One of these practitioners was his dharma successor Ejō. Ejō was two years older than Dōgen and was ordained as a Tendai monk at Mount Hiei. Like Dōgen and other Buddhist leaders, he left the monastery to seek the true way of practice. He studied Pure Land Buddhism and later practiced Zen with Buchi Kakuan, who was a disciple of Dainichi Nōnin, the founder of Nihon Daruma Shū. He received *inka*, or confirmation of enlightenment, from Kakuan. While Dōgen was at Kenninji, Ejō visited him to examine Dōgen

Zenji's dharma. Ejō thought, "I have practiced and accomplished the method of meditation of the Tendai School, have completed the essential practice of Pure Land Buddhism, and have been practicing Zen and attained *kenshō jōbutsu* (seeing nature, becoming buddha). What else does he [Dōgen] have to transmit?" According to the *Denkōroku* (Transmission of light; written by Keizan Jōkin three generations after Dōgen), for the first two or three days everything Dōgen Zenji said agreed with Ejō's understanding, that is, *kensho reichi* (seeing nature as spiritual intelligence). But later, probably because Dōgen Zenji recognized Ejō as a sincere practitioner capable of understanding the true dharma, he started to speak differently. At first Ejō was astonished and tried to argue, but he soon realized that what Dōgen Zenji was saying was much deeper than his own understanding. He aroused *bodhi* (awakened) mind again and desired to practice with Dōgen. But since Dōgen did not have his own monastery, it was impossible. Ejō had to wait until Dōgen founded Kōshōji. He joined Dōgen's sangha in 1234.

It is important to remember that Keizan's *Denkōroku* mentioned that Ejō's understanding of Zen before meeting Dōgen Zenji was *kenshō jōbutsu* or *kenshō reichi*. That is one of the main points of Dōgen Zenji's criticism in *Bendōwa*. In questions seven, ten, sixteen, and seventeen in *Bendōwa*, Dōgen Zenji spoke against this kind of practice. Takeuchi Dōyū, the author of *Eihei niso Koun Ejō Zenji Den* (The biography of Koun Ejō, the second abbot of Eiheiji) has surmised that the eighteen questions and replies in *Bendōwa* were mainly based on the discussion with Ejō at their first meeting at Kenninji.

That is when and why *Bendōwa* was written.

These days *Bendōwa* is considered to be the first chapter of Dōgen's masterwork *Shōbōgenzō* (The true dharma eye treasury), but strictly speaking, *Bendōwa* is not a part of *Shōbōgenzō*. Dōgen Zenji himself compiled *Shichijūgo-kan bon* (the seventy-five-volume version). He wanted to make one hundred chapters, and he wrote twelve more chapters.

That section is called *Jūni-kan bon* (the twelve-volume version). *Bendōwa* was included in neither the seventy-five-volume version nor the twelve-volume version.

Bendōwa was lost and appeared again almost four hundred years later, in the seventeenth century. The political situation in fifteenth- and sixteenth-century Japan was very confused. This period (1477–1573) is called the Warring States period. Japan was not under the control of one government, but divided into many independent states whose people fought each other. Neither the emperor nor the shogun had actual political power. During that time, the vitality of Buddhism declined. Although it spread quietly all over Japan, no eminent masters appeared. Daichi Sokei (1290–1366), who was ordained by Dōgen's disciple Kangan Giin, practiced with Keizan Jōkin, and received transmission from Keizan's successor Meihō Sotetsu, was the last important figure in the lineage of Dōgen Zenji before the Warring States period.

After the Tokugawa Shogunate government was established in the beginning of the seventeenth century, a number of excellent masters appeared. Bannan Eishu (1591–1654) was the first master who tried to reconstruct Dōgen Zenji's way of practice. Kōshōji in Fukakusa was burned soon after Dōgen Zenji left for Echizen (modern Fukui prefecture) and did not exist for about four hundred years until, in 1648, Bannan Eishu rebuilt it at its present location in Uji.

In 1654, shortly after Kōshōji was rebuilt, the Chinese Zen Master Ingen Ryūki (1592–1673) came to Japan with many of his disciples. In 1661 he founded Manpukuji in Uji near Kōshōji. Ingen's teaching was called the Ōbaku School because Ōbaku was the name of the mountain on which he had a monastery in China. (It is also the name of Rinzai's teacher Ōbaku Kiun, Huangbo Xiyun in Chinese.) Ingen Zenji's presence in Japan was very stimulating for Japanese Zen Buddhists. They hoped to find authentic Zen teaching. Since Ingen came from China, the home of Zen, Japanese Buddhists assumed that Ōbaku Zen was authentic Zen.

Many Japanese Rinzai and Sōtō masters visited Ingen and practiced with him, including Gesshū Sōkō (1618–1696). Gesshu was the abbot of Daijōji in Kanazawa, a center of Sōtō Zen at the time, and some of his disciples, such as Manzan Dōhaku (1636–1715) and Tōkuō Ryōkō (1649–1709), were strongly influenced by the Ōbaku style of Zen practice.

After a while people realized that Ōbaku Zen was different from Dōgen Zenji's Zen. For instance, Sonnō Sōeki (1636–1715) criticized Chōon, one of the Ōbaku masters, and said, "Reading the Zazen Ron of Chōon, I understand that in Ming Dynasty China (1368–1644) the practice/enlightenment of the buddha ancestors was lost. If you read this and compare it with Dōgen Zenji's instruction, you will see which is genuine and which is not." (Recorded by Kagamishima Genryū in his *Dōgen Zenji to sono monryu.*) Sonno's dharma successor, Menzan Zuiho (1683–1769), said in his *Jijuyū zanmai,* "That is why some hurry on their way to gain enlightenment by wrestling with koans. Some struggle within themselves, searching for the subject that sees and hears. Some try to rid themselves of their delusory thoughts in order to reach a pleasant place of no-mind, no-thought. Many other methods of practicing zazen were advocated by various teachers in the Song, Yuan, and Ming dynasties in China. However, it appears that fewer than one in a hundred knew the true samadhi transmitted by the buddhas and ancestors."

Sōtō masters tried to research the essence of Dōgen Zenji's teaching. Beside the people mentioned above, Tenkei Denson (1648–1735) was famous for his commentary on the *Shōbōgenzō.*

In the Rinzai school, prominent teachers such as Bankei Yōtaku (1622–1693), Muchaku Dōchu (1653–1744), and Hakuin Ekaku (1685–1768) appeared, starting in the second half of the seventeenth century. Japanese Zen was reconstructed in this period.

Bendōwa was stored at the residence of one of the noble

families in Kyoto, probably Dōgen Zenji's relatives. Menzan described how it was found in his commentary on *Bendōwa*, called *Shōbōgenzō Bendōwa Monge*. A monk whose dharma name was Kannō Sosan used to be a retainer of this family. This man knew that the original text of *Bendōwa* was stored at the family treasury, and he asked to copy the text. Since he knew Gesshū Sōkō, he showed the text to Gesshu who also copied it. Menzan also borrowed the copy from Kannō Sosan and copied it for himself. That was how *Bendōwa* appeared again in this world. When it was published at Eiheiji in the beginning of the nineteenth century, the text was taken as the first chapter of the Honzan version of *Shōbōgenzō*.

Until the Meiji era (1868–1912), some people had doubts about whether or not *Bendōwa* was really written by Dōgen Zenji. Then in 1926 the famous scholar Dōshu Okubo found a different version of *Bendōwa* stored at Shoboji temple in Iwate Prefecture, and he introduced the text. As the Shoboji version was longer, it was a little different from the popular version. The popular version has eighteen questions and answers in the second part, while the Shoboji version has nineteen. Scholars think the Shoboji version was the first draft.

Bokusan Nishiari Zenji (1821–1910), one of the most important Sōtō Zen masters in the Meiji era, thought that *Bendōwa*, *Genjōkōan*, and *Busshō* (Buddha nature) were the most important chapters in *Shōbōgenzō*. Since Nishiari Zenji had great influence among the Sōtō masters and scholars after him, *Bendōwa* has been recognized as one of the most important writings of Dōgen Zenji. Even now, it is considered to be an introduction to *Shōbōgenzō*, although it is not, strictly speaking, a part of that work.

When Dōgen returned from China, he wrote *Fukanzazengi*, in which he showed concisely how to practice zazen and the meaning of zazen practice. He improved and rewrote *Fukanzazengi* again and again until he was at least forty-five or forty-six years old. I think *Fukanzazengi* is

Dōgen Zenji's most important writing. In a sense, *Bendōwa* is a commentary on *Fukanzazengi*. Not only *Bendōwa*, but all of the *Shōbōgenzō* and Dōgen's other writings, can be seen as commentaries on *Fukanzazengi*, in that they are his commentary on the practice of zazen.

Shōbōgenzō explains zazen from many different aspects: the philosophy of what is buddha-dharma, what this world looks like as seen from zazen, what is the structure of our life, and what kind of attitude we should maintain toward zazen practice and daily activities. *Fukanzazengi* is the center of Dōgen's teaching based on zazen. On the foundation of our sitting, we should create our way to encounter each thing in our day-to-day lives. That is what Dōgen described in the *Eihei Shingi*. In the *Tenzo Kyōkun* he used the example of cooking and taught how to encounter food materials, fire, and water. We should see that everything is just a part of ourselves. But the basis of his teaching is *Fukanzazengi*, and he tried to explain what zazen is in order to create monastic life based on zazen. After that, he wrote ninety-five chapters of *Shōbōgenzō*, *Eihei Shingi*, and many other writings. *Bendōwa* is the first of these works.

In *Bendōwa* Dōgen Zenji explains what has been transmitted from buddha to buddha, from Shakyamuni Buddha to himself. That is the jijuyū zanmai that is our zazen. And he discussed the questions people of his time might have asked about zazen.

About the Title Bendōwa

In modern *kanji* (Chinese characters) *bendōwa* is written in this way: (弁道話). This *ben* (弁) is an abbreviation of the old-style kanji (辨); in some texts it is written this way and in other texts it is written like this: (辯). (刀) *katana* means sword, while (力) *chikara* means power or strength. There is only a slight difference in the characers, so this is easily missed. It is difficult to know whether Dōgen Zenji originally wrote (辨) or (辯).

This kanji, (辨), means to cut something into two with a sword, or to separate one thing from another. Thus it also means to analyze, distinguish, or discriminate. (辨) means strength, or to put total energy into doing one thing. If *ben* is (辨), then *bendōwa* means "to distinguish and show the true way from the false way." But if *ben* is this kanji (辨), then *bendōwa* means "to put our whole energy into practicing the Way."

Menzan said in his *Monge* that *ben* means "to distinguish the true way from the false way." However, Dōgen Zenji also wrote *Bendōhō*, which is a part of *Eihei Shingi*. The *hō* in the *Bendōhō* is "dharma," and means the way or method of doing something. In the case of *Bendōwa*, *ben* could be interpreted as "to separate things," because in the question and answer part of the *Bendōwa* Dōgen discusses what is a true way and what is not. But in the case of *Bendōhō*, he did not discuss true and false ways. He just explained how we should practice, day and night. So in the case of *Bendōhō*, *ben* could not be this kanji (辨). Instead, it must mean that we should put all our energy into practice, or that we should practice wholeheartedly. I think in the case of *Bendōwa* the meaning should be the same, so that *bendō* does not mean to separate or analyze things, but "to practice the Way with all our energy."

Wa means a talk or a story, so *bendōwa* means "a talk or discourse about how to practice the Way wholeheartedly."

Next we should understand, "What is the Way?"

Way (*Dō* or *michi* in Japanese, *Dao* in Chinese) is one of the most important words for East Asians. The Way is something of a vague concept because it has various meanings and connotations. Philosophers of different schools have their own understanding of the Way. When we read *Bendōwa*, we should clarify what Dōgen Zenji means by the Way. In order to do this, let us first look at its different connotations.

The Chinese character for Way (道) originally meant a path to reach some place. This part of the kanji, (首) *kubi*, means a part of our body that is above our neck, that is, "head" or "face." And this part of the kanji, (辶) *shinnyu*, shows the action of walking. So the kanji includes the ideas "face" and "walk." That means to walk in a certain direction. You walk in the direction that you face. When you want to go somewhere you have to take a path that leads to your destination. You walk with your own legs in a certain direction toward the place you want to go. That is the original meaning of the character *dao*.

People try to find out the best way, the shortest and easiest way, to get to their destination. And once the best way is found it becomes a kind of method. If a certain way of going to the destination without fail is established and followed by many people, it becomes a rule or regulation. That gives the word the connotation of regulation, law, or social or moral custom. If you walk within this way you are good, but if you stray from the path you are not good. As members of a society, we are requested to follow a certain way.

For Chinese philosophers like Confucius, the Way was not considered merely "a way to go somewhere." They thought that since the sun, the moon, and stars in the sky move regularly, each of them has its own way. Since the four seasons also change in the same way each year, they felt that each and every thing in this universe has its own way. Confucius also thought human beings have a way that we should follow in order to be members of society. That is social morality, the way of human beings. As long as we are human beings we should follow these certain morals, certain ways.

Other philosophers, like Laozi and Zhuangzi, thought the Way should not be man-made or artificial customs, rules, or morality, but that this whole universe is itself the Way. It cannot be named; it cannot be defined. It is like the Chaos mentioned in Zhuangzi. If you try to give it eyes or a nose or mouth, it dies. That is the Way for Daoists. The Way is the naturalness of the whole universe without any man-made distinctions or discriminations.

Those are the two main usages of the word "Way" in Chinese philosophy. When Buddhism was introduced to China from India, this Chinese word was used as a translation for three or more Sanskrit words. The first is *bodhi*, which means awakening or enlightenment, as in one of the translations of *anuttara samyak sambodhi*, supreme awakening, *mujōdō* (無上道). *Mujōdō* means "the supreme way." *Bodhi* was translated as "way" because of the usage of Daoist philosophy. The second Sanskrit word that was translated as *dao* is *marga*, as in *hasshōdō* (八正道), the eightfold correct path. *Marga* means the way we should follow or walk in order to reach *nirvana*. The third Sanskrit word is *gate*, for example *dō* in *rokudō* (六道), which means the six realms of *samsara*.

Once this character was used in Chinese by people who did not know the original meaning in Sanskrit, I think those three meanings were mixed together. *Gate* means the way of deluded sentient beings. *Bodhi* is awakening or enlightenment. And *marga* is the way from delusion to enlightenment. That is how "Way" was used in Buddhist terminology in China and Japan.

When Dōgen Zenji uses this word *dō*, it is an abbreviation of *butsudō* (仏道), buddha way. That means Buddha's enlightenment, or the truth to which Buddha awakened. The day-to-day practice based on or according to reality or truth is also called the way of Buddha, or the way taught by Buddha.

So in a sense, buddha way or *butsudō* is the way to buddha, or to become a buddha. It also means the way Buddha walked. So we follow the way that buddhas and ancestors walked. All buddhas and ancestors walked the same way, and yet the walk of each is unique. Each person has a different way, a different style, a different kind of expression through his or her activities or characteristics.

For example, Dōgen Zenji used the expression *gyōji dōkan* (行持道環). *Gyōji* means "practice," or "protection of practice," *dō* means "way," and *kan* (環) means "circle." He said that *hosshin* (発心) (arousing bodhi mind), *shugyō* (修行) (practice), *bodhi* (awakening), and nirvana are like a circle. This is the Way of Dōgen Zenji. For him, the Way is not simply one direction from starting point to goal; rather, the Way is like a circle. We arouse bodhi mind moment by moment, we practice moment by moment, we become fully aware moment by moment, and we are in nirvana moment by moment. And we continue to do it ceaselessly. Our practice is perfect in each moment and yet we have a direction toward buddha. It is difficult to grasp with the intellect, but that is the Way that Dōgen Zenji refers to in *Bendōwa*.

So our practice is not a kind of training for the sake of making an ignorant person smart, clever, and finally enlightened. Each action, each moment of sitting, is arousing bodhi mind, practice, awakening, and nirvana. Each moment is perfect, and yet within this perfect moment we have a direction, the bodhisattva vows. "However innumerable all beings are, I vow to save them all. However inexhaustible my delusions are, I vow to extinguish them all. However immeasurable the dharma teachings are, I vow to master them all. However endless the Buddha's way is, I vow to follow it." These four bodhisattva vows are our direction within our moment-by-moment practice. And yet each moment is perfect. Since our delusion is inexhaustible, at no time can we eliminate all our delusions. Still we try to do it moment by moment. This trying is itself the manifestation of the buddha way, buddha's enlightenment. But even though we try as hard as possible to do it, we cannot be perfect. So we should repent. And repentance becomes energy to go further, to practice further in the direction of buddha. That is the basis of bodhisattva practice. Our practice is endless. Enlightenment is beginningless.

My teacher, Uchiyama Roshi, says that a bodhisattva is an ordinary person who has a direction toward buddha. "Direction" is the vow to be a buddha.

Each action in our day-to-day lives should be a manifestation of the Way. We practice because we are already in the Way. As Dōgen Zenji said in the first sentence of the *Fukanzazengi*, "The Way is perfect and universal." The Way permeates the whole universe. We never get out of the Way. We are already in the Way. Dōgen Zenji also wrote in the *Gakudō Yojinshū*, "Practitioners of the Way must first of all have faith in the Way. Those who have faith in the buddha way must believe that one is within the Way from the beginning, that one is free from delusive desires, upside-down ways of seeing things, excesses or deficiencies, and mistakes." This is the basis of our practice. Although we are already in the Way, we are deluded and we miss the Way. It is strange, but that is reality. We are in the Way from the beginningless beginning, and yet we are deluded human beings to the endless end. So our practice, our vow, is endless. And if we practice in that way, then each activity, each practice moment by moment, is the perfect manifestation of the buddha way. That is my understanding of *bendō*, practice of the buddha way, or being in the buddha way.

Jijuyū Zanmai

The first sentence, or first paragraph, of *Bendōwa* is one of Dōgen Zenji's most important statements. It reads:

> All buddha-tathagatas together have been simply transmitting wondrous dharma and actualizing anuttara samyak sambodhi for which there is an unsurpassable, unfabricated, wondrous method. This wondrous dharma, which has been transmitted only from buddha to buddha without deviation, has as its criterion jijuyū zanmai.

This is not an opinion, but a decisive statement. There is no way to argue about this for us practitioners of Dōgen Zenji's way. This is the basis of our practice.

All buddha-tathagatas "have been simply transmitting." The Japanese word for "simply transmitting" is *tanden* (単伝). I think this is one of the most important words for understanding Dōgen Zenji's teaching.

Tan means "one." Only one. Not two, not three. Just one; just one transmission. But there are a few ways to understand this. The first is that buddhas and *tathagatas* (those who come and go in thusness or reality; a standard epithet for buddhas) simply transmit the wondrous dharma. This means that each and every buddha-tathagata transmits nothing but this wondrous dharma. This is the only thing they transmit. Also, this transmission takes place from one person to one person. It cannot be transmitted through radio or television or books. This dharma must be transmitted from one buddha to another. Another connotation of this word *tanden* is that the person who transmits and the person who receives the transmission, both the teacher and the disciple, are one, not separate persons. So dharma is not something substantial, like a book, that can be transmitted from someone to someone else. This is dharma, or *myōhō* (妙法).

Myōhō is also an interesting word. Buddha-tathagatas are transmitting myōhō, the "wondrous dharma." This *myō* has many meanings. *Myō* means "something strange," "something curious," also "something we cannot grasp with the intellect." It also means "excellent, wonderful, something that human beings cannot create." It is beyond anything artificial. We cannot grasp it, so it means "strange" for us because we do not understand it. And also, since we cannot create it, we cannot make it by our effort. It is already there, already given. All we can do is say "excellent, wonderful." It is very precious. We cannot create it; we cannot change it or possess it. It is already full of this universe, and we are already given it. That means it is our life.

Our life is part of the universe, and yet we think our life is our own personal belonging. We create our own personal world through our distinctions, our discrimination, our value judgments and definitions. We analyze and put a name or label on it, and put it into categories to make it easy to understand, to make it easy to deal with. That is the man-made world. Our life is created by our karma, that is, by all the experiences from our birth, or even before our birth.

We receive and create a human world. In that sense subject and object, ourselves and the world, are one. The world is created by our karma, or by our discrimination. And within that world, there are subject and object. There is a kind of separation. Although it is one, we think there is separation. "I am not you, you are not me, and this is not human beings, and this is not a sheet of paper." This is how I create the world, separate things, and make them easy to handle. But this kind of world created by our individuality is not myōhō, although myōhō, the wondrous dharma, includes human creations. The power that makes human creations, that is, all our delusion, is also provided from the wondrous dharma. So our creation, our discrimination, our world, is not real. It is like a phantom. It is not substantial. It appears and disappears moment by moment. Yet our life, including our delusions and our discriminations, is a kind of manifestation of reality. But even though it is the manifestation of reality, we are deluded. The fact that we are deluded is the reality for us human beings.

So our practice is not to eliminate our delusion, but to see or to become aware of the fact that we are deluded. Just become aware of it and let go of it. Do not be pulled by the delusions. Then we really become one with the buddha way or wondrous dharma. Even though we are inherently given wondrous dharma, we do not know it. But the fact that we do not know is an aspect of the wondrous dharma. If we could understand or know it, then it would not be wondrous. So in a sense we have doubt as to whether this is really enlightenment, or really the buddha way, or whether we are really in the buddha way from the beginning. Our practice is to let go of this sort of doubt and sit on the basis of the wondrous dharma, the reality including delusions. This is our practice moment by moment.

Wondrous dharma is already given, and yet within our life we have delusions. Delusions mean our individuality, our limitations as individuals, and also egocentricity. We cannot see the universe from the viewpoints of other people;

we can see things only from "my" point of view. I cannot see from your point of view. Even though I think I can understand it, I really cannot see it, because it is not reality for me. Even if I stand in the same place, the way I see things is different from the way you see them. That is because we have karma and are limited as individuals. I cannot see half of the world. If I try to see the dark side, I have to turn my head. Then I cannot see this part. So each moment we can see only part of the world, not the whole world. That is the source of delusion.

In order to see the whole universe we have to get out of the universe. But this is impossible. We are already in the world. We are already standing on a certain point, and we see only part of the world each time. I know that there is an incense stand on the *tokonoma* alcove behind me, but I do not see it now. In this moment, I do not see it, so it is not reality for me. As a memory, I know that it is there. Our own picture of the world is a kind of a fantasy made of our memory in our brain. Each person has this limitation. That is why we have problems, troubles, fighting, arguments. The angles we see the world from are different, and anuttara samyak sambodhi, the supreme awareness, is to see that we cannot see the whole world, to understand that we are deluded and limited. This means we have to let go of our viewpoints. That means we sit on the *zafu* (cushion), we sit in the correct posture, and breathe quietly and let go of thought. Just do zazen. In our sitting we are freed from our limitations by letting go of our limited views. This is the supreme awareness. I do not think supreme awareness or anuttara samyak sambodhi means something we can attain, something we can achieve. But when we let go of our limited view, anuttara samyak sambodhi is there, before or beyond our perception or thought that "I am aware." Just let go of everything, memory or consciousness or whatever. Only when we are actually doing this are we free from the limitations of our individuality.

Our practice of zazen itself is anuttara samyak sambodhi,

and this is what has been transmitted through buddhas and ancestors. And nothing else was transmitted. That is the meaning of *tanden* or "simply transmitted."

The expression of the awareness is different for each person. We should create our own unique way of life. Kōdō Sawaki Roshi said, "The person who left home [a monk] should be a person who creates his own life." This means that each person should create his own unique way of expressing the anuttara samyak sambodhi that is already given. And the way to manifest it should be transmitted from the person who is actually doing it. That is a teacher. So we should have a teacher. The dharma should be transmitted from teacher to student. A teacher is a living example of manifestation of anuttara samyak sambodhi. So anuttara samyak sambodhi is not a kind of concept or something that can be written in a book and given as a secret teaching.

Our own life itself is universal and also unique. Our life is pervading the whole universe, and yet my life is just myself. We cannot share our lives with others. So this universality and individuality is completely present at this moment, and we should create our own way of life, our own way of practice based on that universal reality. That is the wondrous dharma. That is what all buddha-tathagatas are transmitting, and what we are following and trying to practice each moment, day after day, year after year, until the end of our lives. And through our practice, the buddha-dharma manifests and influences other people. This is like a circle. That is what Dōgen Zenji calls *jijuyū zanmai* and describes in the beginning of *Bendōwa*.

Shohaku Okumura
From a lecture at Kōshōji Monastery, Uji, Japan

Talk on Wholehearted Practice of the Way: A Translation of Eihei Dōgen's Bendōwa

All buddha-tathagatas together have been simply transmitting wondrous dharma and actualizing anuttara samyak sambodhi for which there is an unsurpassable, unfabricated, wondrous method.[1] This wondrous dharma, which has been transmitted only from buddha to buddha without deviation, has as its criterion jijuyū zanmai.[2]

For disporting oneself freely in this samadhi, practicing zazen in an upright posture is the true gate.[3] Although this dharma is abundantly inherent in each person, it is not manifested without practice, it is not attained without realization. When you let go, the dharma fills your hands; it is not within the boundary of one or many. When you try to speak, it fills your mouth; it is not limited to vertical or horizontal.[4] Buddhas continuously dwell in and maintain this dharma, yet no trace of conceptualization remains. Living beings constantly function in and use this dharma, yet it does not appear in their perception.

The wholehearted practice of the Way that I am talking about allows all things to exist in enlightenment and enables us to live out oneness in the path of emancipation. When we break through the barrier and drop off all limitations, we are no longer concerned with conceptual distinctions.

After arousing bodhi mind and beginning to seek the dharma, I traveled throughout this country and visited various teachers.[5] During that time I met my late teacher Myōzen at Kenninji temple. Nine years passed swiftly while

I practiced with him, and I learned a little of the way of the Rinzai tradition. Master Myōzen was a great disciple of Ancestor Eisai, from whom he alone received correct transmission of the unsurpassable buddha-dharma.⁶ No one could compare to Myōzen.

Later I went to Song [dynasty] China and visited various masters in Zhejiang Province, where I learned the ways of the five schools of Zen. Finally, I met Zen Master Nyojō on Mount Taipai and completely clarified the great matter of lifelong practice.⁷ After that, I returned home in the first year of Sheting (1227).⁸ To spread this dharma and to free living beings became my vow. I felt as if a heavy burden had been placed on my shoulders.

In spite of that, I set aside my vow to propagate this, in order to wait for conditions under which it could flourish. For now I will live alone, moving from place to place like a cloud or duckweed, and follow the way of the ancient sages. However, there might be some sincere practitioners who on their own do not seek after fame or profit and who give priority to the mind that seeks the Way. But they still may be vainly led astray by false teachers and recklessly cover up correct understanding and become drunk in their own confusion, sinking into delusion for a long time. How will it be possible for [these sincere practitioners] to nurture the true seed of prajna and have appropriate occasion to attain the Way? Since this unworthy wayfarer [Dōgen] is now living like a cloud or duckweed, how will they find the mountain or river where they can visit me? Because I care about these people, I have recollected and written about what I saw with my own eyes of the style of practice in the Zen monasteries of Song China, and what I received and uphold as the profound teaching of my master. I leave this for devoted practitioners of the way of serenity in order to let them know about the true dharma of buddhas. Here is the genuine expression of the essence.

Great Teacher Shakyamuni Buddha imparted the dharma to Mahakashyapa at the Vulture Peak assembly, and it was correctly transmitted from ancestor to ancestor until it reached the venerable Bodhidharma.[9] Bodhidharma himself went to China and imparted the dharma to the Great Teacher Eka.[10] This was the first transmission of the buddha-dharma in the East (China).

In the same manner, the dharma was directly transmitted [ancestor to ancestor] until it eventually reached the Sixth Ancestor, Zen Master Daikan.[11] At that time, the authentic buddha-dharma actually spread throughout China, and reality beyond conceptual distinctions was manifested. There were two great disciples under the Sixth Ancestor: Ejō of Nangaku and Gyōshi of Seigen.[12] Both of them transmitted and maintained buddha mudra and were guiding teachers for all beings.[13] As these two streams of the dharma flowed and permeated widely, the five gates opened: the Hōgen, Igyō, Sōtō, Unmon, and Rinzai schools.[14] These days in Song China, only the Rinzai school is present everywhere. Although the five schools differ, there is only one buddha mind mudra.

In China, although scriptures were continuously introduced and spread since the later Han dynasty (first century B.C.E.), still no one could determine which was most essential. After the First Ancestor came from the West, the roots of the entanglements were cut, and the one buddha-dharma pervaded. We cannot help but yearn for this to happen in our country as well.

For all ancestors and buddhas who have been dwelling in and maintaining buddha-dharma, practicing upright sitting in jijuyū zanmai is the true path for opening up enlightenment.[15] Both in India and in China, those who have attained enlightenment have followed this way. This is because each teacher and each disciple has been intimately and correctly transmitting this subtle method and receiving and maintaining its true spirit.

According to the unmistakenly handed down tradition, the straightforward buddha-dharma that has been simply transmitted is supreme among the supreme. From the time you begin practicing with a teacher, the practices of incense burning, bowing, nembutsu, repentance, and reading sutras are not at all essential; just sit, dropping off body and mind.[16]

When one displays the buddha mudra with one's whole body and mind, sitting upright in this samadhi even for a short time, everything in the entire dharma world becomes buddha mudra, and all space in the universe completely becomes enlightenment.[17] Therefore, it enables buddha-tathagatas to increase the dharma joy of their own original grounds and renew the adornment of the way of awakening. Simultaneously, all living beings of the dharma world in the ten directions and six realms become clear and pure in body and mind, realize great emancipation, and their own original face appears. At that time, all things together awaken to supreme enlightenment and utilize buddha-body, immediately go beyond the culmination of awakening, and sit upright under the kingly bodhi tree.[18] At the same time, they turn the incomparable, great dharma wheel and begin expressing ultimate and unfabricated profound prajna.

There is a path through which the anuttara samyak sambodhi of all things returns [to the person in zazen], and whereby [that person and the enlightenment of all things] intimately and imperceptibly assist each other. Therefore this zazen person without fail drops off body and mind, cuts away previous tainted views and thoughts, awakens genuine buddha-dharma, universally helps the buddha work in each place, as numerous as atoms, where buddha-tathagatas teach and practice, and widely influences practitioners who are going beyond buddha, thereby vigorously exalting the dharma that goes beyond buddha.[19] At this time, because earth, grasses and trees, fences and walls, tiles and pebbles, all things in the dharma realm in ten directions, carry out buddha work, therefore everyone receives the benefit of wind and water movement caused by this functioning, and all are imperceptibly helped by the wondrous and incomprehensible influence of buddha to actualize the enlightenment at hand. Since those who receive and use this water and fire extend the buddha influence of original enlightenment, all who live and talk with these people also share and universally unfold the boundless buddha virtue and they circulate the inexhaustible, ceaseless, incomprehensible, and immeasurable buddha dharma within and without the whole dharma world. However, these various [mutual influences] do not mix into the perceptions of this person sitting, because they take place within stillness without any fabrication, and they are enlightenment itself. If practice and enlightenment were separate as people commonly believe, it would be possible for them to perceive each other.[20] But that which is associated with perceptions cannot be the standard of enlightenment because deluded human sentiment cannot reach the standard of enlightenment.

Moreover, although both mind and object appear and disappear within stillness, because this takes place in the realm of self-receiving and self-employing (*jijuyū*) without moving a speck of dust or destroying a single form, extensive buddha work and profound, subtle buddha influence are carried out.[21] The grass, trees, and earth affected by this functioning radiate great brilliance together and endlessly expound the deep, wondrous dharma. Grasses and trees, fences and walls demonstrate and exalt it for the sake of living beings, both ordinary and sage; and in turn, living beings, both ordinary and sage, express and unfold it for the sake of grasses and trees, fences and walls. The realm of self-awakening and awakening others is fundamentally endowed with the quality of enlightenment with nothing lacking, and allows the standard of enlightenment to be actualized ceaselessly.

Therefore, even if only one person sits for a short time, because this zazen is one with all existence and completely permeates all time, it performs everlasting buddha guidance within the inexhaustible dharma world in the past, present, and future. [Zazen] is equally the same practice and the same enlightenment for both the person sitting and for all dharmas.[22] The melodious sound continues to resonate as it echoes, not only during sitting practice, but before and after striking *sunyata*, which continues endlessly before and after a hammer hits it.[23] Not only that, but all things are endowed with original practice within the original face, which is impossible to measure.

You should know that even if all the buddhas in the ten directions, as numerous as the sands of the Ganges River, together engage the full power of their buddha wisdom, they could never reach the limit, or measure or comprehend the virtue, of one person's zazen.

QUESTION ONE:

Now we have heard that the virtue of this zazen is immense. Stupid people may question this by asking, "There are many gates to the buddha-dharma. Why do you only recommend zazen?"

REPLY:

It is because this is the true gate to buddha-dharma.

QUESTION TWO:

Why is this alone the true gate?

REPLY:

Great Teacher Shakyamuni correctly transmitted the wondrous method for attaining the Way, and the tathagatas of the three times (past, present, and future) also all attain the Way through zazen. For this reason, [zazen] has been conveyed from one person to another as the true gate. Not only that, but all the ancestors of India and China attained the Way through zazen. Therefore I am now showing the true gate to human and celestial beings.

QUESTION THREE:

Relying on either the correct transmitting of the wondrous method of tathagatas or following the tracks of the ancestral teachers is truly beyond our ordinary thinking. However, reading sutras or chanting nembutsu naturally can become a cause of satori. How can just sitting vainly without doing anything be a means for attaining enlightenment?

REPLY:

That you now consider the samadhi of the buddhas, the unsurpassed great dharma, as vainly sitting doing nothing, is slandering the Mahayana. This is very deep delusion, as if saying that there is no water even while being in the middle of the great ocean. Thankfully, [doing zazen] is already sitting peacefully in the jijuyū zanmai of the buddhas. Doesn't this manifest extensive virtue? It is pitiful that your eyes are not yet open and your mind is still drunk.

On the whole, the buddha realm is incomprehensible, unreachable through discrimination, much less can it be known with no faith and inferior insight. Only people of great capacity and true faith are able to enter. People without faith have difficulty accepting, even when taught. Even at Vulture Peak, there was a group of people of whom Buddha said, "It is good that they leave."[24] Generally, if true faith arises in your heart, you should practice and study. If it does not, you should give it up for a while and regret not having the blessing of dharma from long ago.

Furthermore, do you really know the virtue to be gained by working at such practices as reading sutras or chanting nembutsu? The notion that merely making sounds by moving your tongue leads to the virtue of the buddha work is completely meaningless; it is extremely far, tremendously distant, from resembling buddha-dharma. Also, as for opening the sutras, if you clearly understand what Buddha has taught as the principle of sudden and gradual practice, and practice in accord with that teaching, you will certainly accomplish enlightenment. Vainly wasting your thinking and discrimination does not compare to the virtue of gaining bodhi. Intending to reach the buddha way through stupid ceaseless chanting millions of times is like steering a cart north and trying to go south. It is also the

same as trying to put a square peg in a round hole. Reading
literature while ignoring the way of practice is like a person
reading a prescription but forgetting to take the medicine;
what is the benefit? Continuously uttering sounds like frogs
in a spring rice paddy croaking day and night is also ultimately worthless. Furthermore, people deeply blinded by
fame and profit have difficulty abandoning these things
because their greed is exceedingly deep. Since this was the
case in ancient times, why shouldn't it be so in the modern
world? We must feel the utmost sympathy.

You must clearly understand that the wondrous dharma
of the seven buddhas manifests its essential meaning and is
received and upheld only when a practitioner matches the
mind, actualizes awakening, and follows and receives the true
transmission of a master who embodies the Way and clarifies
the mind.[25] This [wondrous dharma] cannot be fully understood by a teacher who only studies words. Therefore, immediately cease this skepticism, practice the way of zazen under
the guidance of a true teacher, and fully actualize the jijuyū
zanmai of the buddhas.

QUESTION FOUR:

The Hokke (Tendai) and Kegon teachings, which have
been transmitted now in our country, are both the most sublime teachings of the Mahayana.[26] Moreover, the Shingon
teaching was intimately transmitted from Vairocana
Tathagata to Vajrasattva, from teacher to disciple without
deviation.[27] Its principle is that "Mind itself is buddha" or
"This mind becomes buddha," which propounds the true
awakening of the five buddhas at the instant of sitting, without passing through many *kalpas* of practice.[28] This must be
called the pinnacle of buddha-dharma. In spite of that, what
superior features in the practice you are now speaking about
cause you to recommend this only and set aside those others?

REPLY:

Buddhist practitioners should know not to argue
about the superiority or inferiority of teachings and not to

discriminate between superficial or profound dharma, but should only know whether the practice is genuine or false. There were those who flowed into the buddha way drawn by grasses, flowers, mountains, or rivers, and there are some who received and upheld the buddha mudra from grasping earth, stones, sand, or pebbles. Furthermore, words that express the vastness [of reality] are even more abundant than all the myriad things, but also the turning of the great dharma wheel is contained in one speck of dust. Therefore, the words "The mind itself is buddha" are like the moon reflected in the water. The principle "at the instant of sitting becoming buddha" is also a reflection within a mirror. Don't be caught up in the skillfulness of words. Now, in order to allow you to become an authentic person of the Way, I recommend [truly engaging in] practice that directly actualizes bodhi, and am showing you the wondrous way that is simply transmitted by buddha ancestors.

Also, in transmitting buddha-dharma, you must definitely have as a true teacher someone who accords with enlightenment. It is worthless to take as a guiding teacher a scholar who just makes calculations about words, since this would be like a blind person leading the blind. Now, the followers of the authentic transmission of buddha ancestors all esteem the clear-sighted masters who have attained the way and accord with enlightenment, and request them to maintain buddha-dharma. Because of this, deities from seen and unseen realms who come to take refuge, as well as people who have actualized the rank of *arhat* and come to ask about the dharma, will all without fail be given the means to clarify the mind ground.[29] We have not yet heard about this in the various schools. Buddha disciples should just learn buddha-dharma.

You should also know that we unquestionably lack nothing of unsurpassed bodhi, but although we receive and use it endlessly, because we cannot fully accept it we mindlessly make our arising views habitual and think of this [buddha-dharma] as an object, thus vainly stumbling on the great way. Because of these views, people see various [illusory] flowers in the sky, such as believing [buddha's teaching to be only] the twelve-fold chain of causation of the twenty-five realms of existence, or never exhausting the doctrines of three vehicles, five vehicles, and buddha's existence or nonexistence.[30] These views arise endlessly. You should not think that studying such teachings is the correct way to practice buddha-dharma.[31] On the contrary, when we truly do zazen thoroughly, relying on the buddha mudra and letting go of all affairs, we transcend the limits of sentimental judgments about delusion and enlightenment, are not caught up in the [dichotomy of] paths of ordinary people or sages, and immediately stroll beyond classifications and receive and use great awakening.[32] How can the activities of those who are involved in the snares of words and phrases compare with this?

QUESTION FIVE:

Concentration is one of the three basic studies; meditation is one of the six *paramitas*.[33] Both of these are studied by all bodhisattvas from the beginning and practiced regardless of whether they are sharp or dull. So the zazen you now speak of is already included. For what reason do you say the true dharma of the tathagata is consolidated in this [one practice]?

REPLY:

This question is arising now because you name as "Zen School" this unsurpassed great dharma of the true dharma eye treasury, the one great matter of the tathagatas.[34] You should know that this title "Zen School" originated in China and was never heard of in India. At first, while Great Master Bodhidharma sat facing the wall for nine years at Shōrinji Temple on Su Mountain, both monks and laypeople did not yet know buddha's true dharma and called him the brahman who practiced zazen as the essence.[35] After that, all the ancestors for each generation always just practiced zazen. Seeing this, foolish worldly people, who did not understand the reality, in confusion called this the "Zazen School."[36] Nowadays, they omit the word *za* (sitting) and just call it the "Zen School." This process is obvious from the sayings of the ancestors. Do not consider [zazen] to be the concentration and meditation of the six paramitas and the three basic studies.

The intention of Buddha to transmit this buddha-dharma is revealed in his own life. It is useless to doubt the truth that the ceremony done by the Tathagata in ancient times at the assembly on Vulture Peak, when he transmitted solely to Venerable Mahakashyapa the unsurpassed great dharma of the true dharma eye treasury of the wondrous mind of nirvana, was seen with their own eyes by celestial beings presently in the heavenly realms.[37] Definitely the buddha-dharma is protected eternally by those celestial beings, whose guardianship has not yet passed. Truly you should know that this [zazen] is the complete path of the buddha-dharma, and nothing can compare with it.

QUESTION SIX:

Among the four different postures (walking, standing, sitting, lying down), why does Buddhism encourage entering realization through meditation only in sitting?

REPLY:

It is not possible to thoroughly comprehend the path by which the buddhas from the past, one after another, have been practicing and entering realization. If you seek a reason, you must know that it is only because [sitting] is what has been used by Buddhist practitioners, and beyond this you do not need to search. However, the Ancestor [Nagarjuna] praises it, saying "Zazen itself is the dharma gate of ease and delight (nirvana)."[38] So couldn't we infer that it is because [sitting] is the most stable and peaceful of the four postures? Moreover, this is not the path of practice of one or two buddhas, but all buddhas and ancestors follow this path.

QUESTION SEVEN:

As for the practice of zazen, people who have not yet realized buddha-dharma should attain enlightenment through practicing the way of zazen.[39] But what could those who have already clarified the true buddha-dharma expect from doing zazen?

REPLY:

Although it is said that one should not relate dreams to fools and it is useless to give oars to mountain folks, I will give you further instruction.

Thinking that practice and enlightenment are not one is no more than a view that is outside the Way [that is, deluded]. In buddha-dharma, practice and enlightenment are one and the same. Because it is the practice of enlightenment, a beginner's wholehearted practice of the Way is exactly the totality of original enlightenment. For this reason, in conveying the essential attitude for practice, it is taught not to wait for enlightenment outside practice. This must be so because [this practice] is the directly indicated original enlightenment. Since it is already the enlightenment of practice, enlightenment is endless; since it is the practice of enlightenment, practice is beginningless. Therefore, both Shakyamuni Tathagata and Venerable Mahakashyapa were accepted and used in the practice of enlightenment, and in the same manner Great Teacher Bodhidharma and Great Ancestor Daikan [the Sixth Ancestor] were pulled and turned in the practice of enlightenment. Traces of dwelling in and maintaining buddha-dharma are all like this.

Already there is practice not separate from enlightenment, and fortunately for us, this wholehearted engaging the Way with beginner's mind, which transmits the undivided wondrous practice, is exactly attaining undivided original enlightenment in the ground of nonfabrication. We must know that, in order not to allow defilement of enlightenment inseparable from practice, the buddha ancestors vigilantly teach us not to slacken practice.[40] When wondrous practice is cast off original enlightenment fills our hands; when we are free from original enlightenment wondrous practice is carried out through the whole body.

Also, I saw with my own eyes in Great Song China that Zen monasteries in various regions, with from five or six hundred to one or two thousand monks, all had zazen halls and doing zazen day and night was encouraged. When I asked the teachers transmitting buddha mind mudra and who were in charge of temples about the essence of buddha-dharma, they spoke of the principle that practice and enlightenment are not two.

For this reason I urge not only the practitioners in this tradition but all lofty persons seeking dharma, people wishing for the genuine buddha-dharma regardless of whether they are beginners or advanced, without distinguishing between the ordinary and the sage, to engage in zazen according to the teachings of the buddha ancestors and following the path of masters.

Haven't you heard the ancestral teacher's utterance, "It is not that there is no practice and enlightenment, but only that it cannot be defiled"? Also it was said, "A person who sees the Way practices the Way."[41] You should know that you must practice in the midst of attaining the Way.

QUESTION EIGHT:

When all the teachers who spread the teachings in our country in past ages came back from China and introduced Buddhism, why did they put aside this essential practice and only bring back the teachings?

REPLY:

The reason the ancient teachers did not convey this practice is that the time was not yet ripe.

QUESTION NINE:

Did those venerable teachers comprehend this dharma?

REPLY:

If they had understood, it would have been introduced.

QUESTION TEN:

Someone has said, "Do not grieve over life and death. There is an instantaneous means for separating from life and death. It is to understand the principle that mind nature is permanent. This means that even though the body that is born will inevitably be carried into death, still this mind nature never perishes. If you really understand that the mind nature existing in our body is not subject to birth and death, then since it is the original nature, although the body is only a temporary form haphazardly born here and dying, the mind is permanent and unchangeable in the past, present, and future. To know this is called release from life and death. Those who know this principle will forever extinguish their rounds of life and death, and when their bodies perish they enter into the ocean of original nature. When they stream into this ocean, they are truly endowed with the same wondrous virtues as the buddha-tathagatas. Now even though you know this, because your body was produced by the delusory karma of previous lives, you are not the same as the sages. Those who do not yet know this must forever transmigrate within the realm of life and death. Consequently, you need comprehend only the permanence of mind nature. What can you expect from vainly spending your whole life doing quiet sitting?"

Is such an opinion truly in accord with the way of buddhas and ancestors?

REPLY:

The idea you have just mentioned is not buddha-dharma at all, but the fallacious view of Senika.[42]

This fallacy says that there is a spiritual intelligence in one's body which discriminates love and hatred or right and wrong as soon as it encounters phenomena, and has the capacity to distinguish all such things as pain and itching or suffering and pleasure. Furthermore, when this body perishes, the spirit nature escapes and is born elsewhere. Therefore, although it seems to expire here, since [the spirit-nature] is born somewhere, it is said to be permanent, never perishing. Such is this fallacious doctrine.

However, to learn this theory and suppose it is buddha-dharma is more stupid than grasping a tile or a pebble and thinking it is a golden treasure. Nothing can compare to the shamefulness of this idiocy. National Teacher Echū of Tang China strictly admonished [against this mistake].[43] So now isn't it ridiculous to consider that the erroneous view of mind as permanent and material form as impermanent is the same as the wondrous dharma of the buddhas, and to think that you become free from life and death when actually you are arousing the fundamental cause of life and death? This indeed is most pitiful. Just realize that this is a mistaken view. You should give no ear to it.

Since I cannot avoid this issue, I must now further bestow compassion and extricate you from this false view. You should know that fundamentally in buddha-dharma it is affirmed that body and mind are one, essence and material form are not two, and you should have no doubt whatsoever that this is similarly understood in India and in China. Moreover, in the gate of speaking of permanence, all the ten thousand dharmas are permanent, body and mind are not separate. In the gate of speaking about impermanence all dharmas are impermanent, essence and material form are not separate.[44] Why do you call the body impermanent and the mind permanent contrary to the true principle? Not only that, you should completely awaken to life and death as exactly nirvana. You can never speak of nirvana as outside life and death. Furthermore, although you have the illusory idea that the understanding that mind is permanent and apart from the body is the buddha wisdom distinct from life and death, still the mind with this discriminating view is itself arising and perishing, not permanent at all. Isn't this [illusory idea] insignificant?

You must savor that the principle of oneness of body

and mind is just the everyday talk of buddha-dharma. How then, when this body ceases to exist, could the mind alone leave the body and not cease to exist? If there is a time when they are one and a time when they are not one, then the Buddha's words would unavoidably become vain and false. Also, thinking that life and death must be eliminated, you are guilty of hating buddha-dharma. Why don't you be careful?

You should understand that in buddha-dharma, what is called the dharma gate of the vast total aspect of mind essence includes the whole vast dharma realm without separating essence and appearance and without speaking of arising and ceasing.[45] [From life and death] up to and including bodhi and nirvana, there is nothing that is not mind essence. Without exception, all the myriad phenomena in the entire universe are nothing other than this one mind, with everything included and interconnected. These various dharma gateways are all equally this one mind. Saying there is no difference at all [between essence and appearance] is exactly how Buddhists understand mind essence.

Consequently, in this one-dharma, how could you discriminate between body and mind or separate life and death from nirvana? As you are already Buddha's child, do not listen to the blabbering of maniacs who preach this fallacious view.

QUESTION ELEVEN:

Is it necessary for those who focus on this zazen to observe the precepts strictly?

REPLY:

The sacred practice of maintaining the precepts is indeed the guiding rule of the Zen gate and the traditional style of buddhas and ancestors, but even those who have not yet received precepts or who have broken the precepts still do not lack the possibility [to practice zazen].[46]

QUESTION TWELVE:

Will it be a problem if people who work diligently at

this zazen also combine it with practicing shingon or *shikan*?[47]

REPLY:

When I was in China and had a chance to ask my teacher about the essence, he said he had never heard that the ancestors who properly transmitted buddha mudra from ancient to present times in India and China had ever combined practices like that. Truly, if you do not engage in one thing, you will never reach one wisdom.[48]

QUESTION THIRTEEN:

Can this practice be carried out also by male and female laypeople, or can it only be practiced by monks?

REPLY:

The Ancestral Teachers stated that in attaining buddhadharma there is no distinction between men and women, or noble and common.

QUESTION FOURTEEN:

Monks quickly depart from their involvements and have no obstacles to wholeheartedly engaging in the way of zazen. But how can people who are busy with their duties in the world single-mindedly practice and be in accord with the buddha way of non-action?

REPLY:

Certainly the buddha ancestors with their great sympathy keep open the vast gate of compassion in order to allow all living beings to enter enlightenment. So which of the various beings would not enter?

If we search, there are many examples of this from antiquity to the present. For instance, although the Emperors Daisō and Junso were fully occupied with many functions during their reigns, they diligently practiced zazen and were proficient in the great way of the buddha ancestors.[49] Also Prime Ministers Ri and Bo, although they served in positions as imperial aides and were highly trusted retainers of

emperors, diligently practiced zazen and entered the enlightenment of the great way of buddha ancestors.[50] This
only depends on whether or not one has aspiration, without
relationship to being a monk or layperson. Also, anyone who
can deeply discern what is important or trivial will thereby
have this faith. Needless to say, people who think secular
duties interfere with buddha-dharma only know that there is
no buddha-dharma in the secular realm, and do not yet realize that there is nothing secular in the realm of buddha.

Recently in China there was a minister of state named
Hou, a high official who was experienced in the Ancestral
Way.[51] He wrote a poem expressing himself:

> *In my spare time from state affairs I enjoy zazen,*
> *and hardly sleep lying down on the bed.*
> *Although still manifesting the appearance of a government*
> *official,*
> *My name has pervaded the four oceans as a senior adept.*

Although this person had no rest from his official
duties, because of his deep aspiration he attained the buddha
way. Seeing others, examine yourself; reflect the ancient in
the present.

In Great Song China nowadays the Emperor and great
ministers, educated and common people, men and women,
all are attentive to the Ancestral Way. Military and civilian
officials all aspire to study the Way in Zen practice. Of those
who so aspire, many will certainly open and clarify the mind
ground. Obviously this shows that secular duties do not
obstruct buddha-dharma.

If the genuine buddha-dharma permeates the country,
because of the ceaseless protection of buddhas and heavenly
beings, the emperor's reign will be peaceful. If the reign is
peaceful, buddha-dharma attains its strength.

Also, during Shakyamuni's stay in the world, even the
worst criminals and those with harmful views gained the
Way. In the assemblies of ancestral teachers, even hunters
and woodcutters realized *satori*.[52] Needless to say, other
people can do this. Just seek the guidance of a true teacher.

QUESTION FIFTEEN:

Even in this corrupt declining age of the world, is it possible to attain enlightenment through this practice?[53]

REPLY:

In the Teaching Schools they focus on various classification systems, yet in the true teaching of Mahayana there is no distinction of True, Semblance, and Final Dharma, and it is said that all who practice will attain the Way. Especially in this simply transmitted true dharma, both in entering dharma and in embodying it freely, we receive and use our own family treasure. Only those who practice know on their own whether they attain enlightenment or not, just as those who use water notice on their own if it is cold or warm.

QUESTION SIXTEEN:

Someone said, "In buddha-dharma, those who thoroughly understand the principle that mind itself is buddha, even if they do not chant sutras with their mouths or practice the buddha way with their bodies, still lack nothing at all of buddha-dharma. Simply knowing that the buddha-dharma exists in the self from the beginning is the perfect accomplishment of the Way. Outside of this, you should not seek from other people, much less take the trouble to engage the Way in zazen."

REPLY:

These words are total nonsense. If it is as you said, how could anyone with cognition fail to understand when taught this principle?

You should know that buddha-dharma is studied by truly giving up the view that discriminates between self and others. If just knowing that the self is itself buddha was attainment of the Way, Shakyamuni would not have taken the trouble in ancient times to give guidance. Now I will confirm this with an excellent example from an ancient worthy.

Long ago, Gensoku was the director monk in the assembly of Zen Master Hōgen.[54] Hōgen asked him,

"Director Gensoku, how long have you been in my assembly?"

Gensoku replied, "I have already been in the Master's assembly for three years."

Hōgen said, "You are a student. Why haven't you ever asked me about buddha-dharma?"

Gensoku said, "I cannot deceive you, O teacher. Once when I was at Zen Master Seihō's place, I realized the peace and joy of buddha-dharma."[55]

Hōgen asked, "With which words were you able to enter?"

Gensoku responded, "I once asked Seihō, 'What is the self of the student [that is, my own self]?' Seihō said, 'The fire boy comes seeking fire.'"[56]

Hōgen said, "Good words! However, I'm afraid that you did not really understand them."

Gensoku said, "My understanding is that the fire boy belongs to fire. Already fire, still he seeks fire, just like being self and seeking self."

Hōgen exclaimed, "Now I really know that you don't understand. If buddha-dharma was like that it would not have been transmitted up to today."

At this, Gensoku was overwrought and left immediately. On the road he thought, "The Master is one of the world's fine teachers, and also the guiding teacher of five hundred people. Certainly there must be merit in his pointing out my error."

He returned to Hōgen and, after doing prostrations in repentance, asked, "What is the self of this student?"

Hōgen said, "The fire boy comes seeking fire." With these words, Gensoku was greatly enlightened to buddha-dharma.[57]

Understand clearly that to comprehend "The self is itself buddha" cannot be called understanding buddha-dharma. If the comprehension that self is itself buddha was the buddha-dharma, Zen Master Hōgen would not have used that saying for guidance or made such an admonishment.

From the time you first meet a good teacher, just genuinely inquire about the manners and standards for practice, single-mindedly engage in the way of zazen, and do not keep your mind stuck on a single knowledge or half comprehension. The wondrous method of buddha-dharma is not without meaning.

QUESTION SEVENTEEN:

We hear that through the ages in India and China, someone was enlightened to the Way by hearing the sound of bamboo, and another clarified the heart on seeing the color of blossoms. Needless to say, Great Teacher Shakyamuni Buddha certified the Way upon seeing the morning star, and Venerable Ananda clarified the dharma when the banner pole [signalling dharma meetings] toppled.[58] Not only that, but among the Five Houses after the Sixth Ancestor many people clarified the mind ground with a single word or half phrase. Were they definitely only people who had engaged the way of zazen?

REPLY:

You should know that, through the ages, those who clarified mind by seeing colors or actualized the Way by hearing sounds were each the exact person who exerted the Way without vacillating deliberation, and right away they had no secondary person [or dualistic being].

QUESTION EIGHTEEN:

In the Western Heaven [India] and in China, people are inherently straightforward. On account of its being the Central Flower [of civilization, i.e., China], when buddha-dharma was expounded they understood very quickly. In our country, from ancient times people have lacked benevolence and wisdom, so shouldn't we regret that, because of being barbarians, it is difficult for us to grow the true seed? Also, home-leaving monks in this country are inferior even to laypeople of those great countries. Everybody here is stupid and narrow-minded. They deeply cling to artificial merits and admire superficial virtues. Even if such people do zazen, how could they actually achieve buddha-dharma?

REPLY:

As you say, benevolence and wisdom have not yet spread to people of our country, who are moreover ignorant and twisted. Even if the authentic dharma was shown, the sweet dew [of Buddha's teaching] would instead become poison. They find it easy to seek fame and profit, and have difficulty dissolving deluded attachments. On the other hand, actualizing and entering buddha-dharma or sailing beyond delusion does not necessarily depend on the intelligence of the human and heavenly realms. Even when the Buddha was in this world, someone attained the fourth stage [of arhat] because of [being hit by] a handball, while another realized the great way through putting on an *okesa* (priest's robe), although both were imbecilic and stupid beasts.[59] However, when assisted by right faith, a pathway for departing delusion does exist.[60] Furthermore, seeing a senile old monk sitting silently, a woman with deep faith who had offered him a meal thereby opened up satori. This was not due to intelligence or from learning, but without waiting for words or sermons she was assisted only by her true faith.[61]

Also, it is only for about two thousand and some years that Shakyamuni's teaching has permeated the three thousand worlds.[62] Among these various lands, all are not necessarily countries of benevolence and wisdom, and the people are not necessarily only intelligent and brilliant. However, the true dharma of the tathagatas, endowed from the beginning with the inconceivably great power of merit and virtue, flourished in those lands as the times matured. If people genuinely practice with right faith, they all attain the Way equally, without distinction between the dull and the sharp-witted. Our country may not be a land of benevolence and wisdom, and the people's understanding may be foolish, but do not think that they cannot realize buddha-dharma. Without question, all people are abundantly endowed with the true seeds of prajna, only they rarely accept it and have not yet received and used it.

The foregoing mutual exchange of questions and answers between guest and host has been disordered and may be confusing. How many flowers have been created in the flowerless sky? However, the essential meaning of engaging the way of zazen has not yet been transmitted in this country, so people who aspire to know it must be sorrowful. For this reason, I have compiled some of what I saw and heard in foreign lands, and have written and preserved my brilliant teacher's true essence in order to make it heard by aspiring practitioners. Besides this, I do not have a chance now to also present the standards for monasteries or the regulations for temples, especially as they should not be treated carelessly.

Indeed, although our country is located to the east of the Dragon Ocean, far away through the clouds and mist, since the time of the Emperors Kinmei and Yōmei the buddha-dharma from the West has moved east, much to everyone's happiness.[63] And yet philosophical categories and religious activities are overgrown and entangled, so that people are unhealthy in their practice. [Instead of that,] now by using ragged robes and old, repaired bowls till the end of this life, tying together a thatched hut by the blue cliffs and white rocks, and practicing upright sitting, the matter going beyond buddha will be instantly manifested and the great matter of the study of one lifetime will be immediately fulfilled. This is precisely the admonition of Ryūge and the style passed on at Kukkutupada.[64] The manner of this zazen should accord with the *Fukanzazengi*, which I formulated in the Karoku Period (1225–1227).[65]

Furthermore, although the spread of buddha-dharma throughout the country should await the emperor's approval, if we consider again the request [of Shakyamuni] at Vulture Peak, then emperors, nobles, ministers, and generals now appearing in a thousand trillion lands have all gratefully received Buddha's approval and have come to be born because they did not forget their dedication, through many lifetimes, to protect buddha-dharma. Which of the regions where their control has extended is not a buddha land?

Consequently, in circulating the way of the buddhas and ancestors, we should not necessarily be selective about places or wait upon conditions. Only do not think that today is the beginning [of our spreading the dharma].

For this reason, I have compiled this writing to leave for bright students who wish to actualize buddha-dharma and for sincere practitioners who wander from place to place like clouds or duckweed seeking the Way.

The third year of the Kangi Period (1231),
on the Mid-autumn Day,
written by Shamon Dōgen who went to China
and who transmits the Dharma.[66]

Notes

1. *Tathagata* is one of the ten epithets for Buddha; it literally means "thus come, thus gone." It is used together with *buddha* for emphasis.

"Simply transmitting" is *tanden* (巣伝), literally single or simple transmission, which implies that the transmission is direct between buddhas, that only the dharma is transmitted, and that it is transmitted completely.

Anuttara samyak sambodhi is incomparable awareness, the supreme enlightenment of Buddha. "Wondrous dharma" is *myōhō* (妙法); *myō* means "wondrous, subtle, excellent, ungraspable"; *dharma* refers to truth or reality, the elements or objects of reality, or the teaching about reality. *Myōhō* is one translation of *saddharma*. *Saddharma* is also translated as *shōbō*, true dharma, the *shōbō* of Dōgen's masterwork *Shōbōgenzō*.

The "wondrous method," *myōjutsu*, might also be translated as "subtle craft." Although this practice might be said to have a method, craft, or criterion, this term as used here by Dōgen is provocative and even ironic, as it is not a method or technique to arrive at some dualistic result not already present, and is not separate from the "wondrous dharma" itself.

2. *Jijuyū zanmai* is literally the "samadhi of self-fulfillment" or "self–enjoyment," or the "samadhi of self receiving or accepting its function." *Ji* is "self"; *juyu* as a common compound means "fulfillment or enjoyment." *Ju* alone is "receive" or "accept"; *yū* alone is "function" or "use." *Zanmai* is samadhi, or concentration. So we can understand this samadhi of self-fulfillment and enjoyment as the samadhi or concentration on the self when it simply receives and accepts its function, or its spiritual position in the world. The important point is that this is not the self that has an object. There is nothing other than or outside of this self. The enjoyment, fulfillment, or satisfaction is the samadhi of the self, of which there is no other. This is not an experience that is somewhere other than here and now, it is not something to be acquired or gained. *Jijuyū* is often contrasted with *tajuyū*, others receiving the enjoyment of dharma. Historically, *tajuyū* refers to other beings receiving the benefits of bodhisattva practice. In the case of Dōgen Zenji's *jijuyū*, there is no *ta*. *Ta* is included in *ji*. Everything becomes everything, all becomes all. *Jijuyū* samadhi is buddha's practice. In *Shōbōgenzō Genjōkōan*, Dōgen Zenji says, "To study the buddha way is to study the Self; to study the Self is to forget the self; to forget the self is to be enlightened by myriad dharmas; to be enlightened by myriad dharmas is to drop off the body and mind of self and others." This is jijuyū zanmai. This actually occurs in zazen.

3. "Disporting oneself freely," *yuge* (遊戲), could also be translated as "play freely." The characters in a later version of the text are *yuke* (遊化), which means "to go out and expound the teaching."

4. "It fills your mouth" could be understood in two ways: the

dharma fills your mouth so that you cannot speak, or the dharma fills your mouth so that whatever you say is the expression of dharma.

5. Bodhi-mind—*bodhicitta* in Sanskrit, *bodaishin* (菩提心) in Japanese—means the mind that seeks awakening.

6. Butsuji Myōzen (1184–1225) was Dōgen's first Zen teacher. Myōzen accompanied Dōgen to China to study, and died there before Dōgen's return. Myōan Eisai (1141–1215) first brought Rinzai Zen to Japan.

7. Tendō Nyojō, (1163–1228, Tiantong Rujing in Chinese) transmitted the Sōtō lineage (Caodong in Chinese) to Dōgen.

8. Sheting, a Chinese era name, is pronounced *Shōtei* in Japanese.

9. Shakyamuni Buddha (fifth century B.C.E.); Mahakashyapa, a disciple of Shakyamuni, was considered to be the First Ancestor of Zen. Vulture Peak was the site in Northern India where Shakyamuni spoke the Lotus Sutra. Bodhidharma (fifth–sixth century C.E.), Twenty-eighth Ancestor from Mahakashyapa, is considered the First Ancestor of Zen in China.

10. Taiso Eka (487–593, Dazu Huike in Chinese).

11. Daikan Enō (638–713, Dajian Huineng in Chinese).

12. Nangaku Ejō (677–744, Nanyue Huairang in Chinese); Seigen Gyōshi (660–740, Qingyuan Xingsi). The Rinzai lineage eventually derived from Nangaku, the Sōtō tradition from Seigen.

13. *Mudra* is Sanskrit for "seal," as in seal or stamp of approval. This term is also used for specific postures or gestures. Here it represents the embodiment of the awakened mind.

14. The classical five houses of Zen are Hōgen, Igyō, Sōtō, Unmon, and Rinzai in Japanese, and Fayan, Guiyang, Caodong, Yunmen, and Linji in Chinese.

15. The section beginning with this sentence, "For all ancestors and buddhas who have been dwelling in and maintaining buddha–dharma . . ." and going to the first

question below is chanted daily as a separate text in Sōtō Zen temples and referred to as the Jijuyū Zanmai, or Samadhi of Self–fulfillment.

16. Nembutsu was originally the practice of chanting the name and visualizing the image of any buddha or buddha land, and only later, in Pure Land Buddhism, came to mean chanting the name of Amitabha; repentance, *shusan* (修 讖) in Japanese, refers to the *fusatsu* (*posadha* in Sanskrit), a ceremony of repentance and taking vows and refuge that occurs regularly in Buddhist communities. "Dropping off body and mind" is an important term for Dōgen. Dōgen indicates here that these practices should come from *shinjin datsuraku* (dropping off body and mind), in other words zazen; they should be expressions of *shikantaza* (just sitting); otherwise they are meaningless.

This could also be read literally as "From the time you begin practicing with a teacher, do not use [these practices]; just sit, dropping off body and mind. . . ." This is to say that such practices should not be *used as instruments* to attain spiritual advancement. Rather, they should be enacted as expressions of self–fulfilling samadhi. In his own practice Dōgen continued to engage in all of these specific practice activities with this attitude.

17. "Whole body and mind" is literally "body, speech, and mind." This complex passage, beginning "When one displays the buddha mudra, . . ." reflects the non–anthropocentric basis of Buddhist thought and practice. The active realization embodied and supported in self–fulfilling samadhi includes not only humans and other creatures, but even the land and soil, and the "grasses and trees, fences and walls, tiles and pebbles" Dōgen mentions below. Even things usually considered inanimate objects in Western philosophy vitally partake of this awakening and mutually resonate to encourage the subtle, mysterious buddha guidance or influence in all of us. This Buddhist view of our

environment and all the things that make it up as alive and intimately connected with us rather than a collection of dead objects, has become of great interest to modern thinkers concerned with the threats of environmental degradation and the underlying attitudes that have helped endanger our ecology.

18. The six realms are hell, the realms of hungry ghosts, of animals, of *asuras* (titans), of human beings, and of heavenly beings. "Supreme enlightenment" in this sentence is *Shōgaku* (正覚) in Japanese; this refers to anuttara samyak sambodhi.

19. "Each place" is *dōjō* (道場), a place where buddha-tathagatas practice and manifest the buddha-dharma.

20. The somewhat ambiguous phrase, "It would be possible for them to perceive each other," might be interpreted as "It should be possible for practice and enlightenment to be perceived separately."

21. "Mind and object" could be understood as subject and object. "Appear and disappear" is a translation of *shō nyū go shutsu* (証入悟出), literally "enlightened entering and enlightened leaving."

22. Dōgen says literally, "Equal same practice and same enlightenment for both this and that." The understood subject is zazen, or the whole activity of buddha work which Dōgen has been describing. We have translated "this and that" or "it, it" as "the person sitting and all dharmas." However, these words may also imply the distinction of ordinary people and sages, as well as that of subject and object represented by the person sitting and all phenomena.

23. *Sunyata* is literally "empty space." Dōgen refers to the Buddhist teaching of *sunyata*, sometimes translated as emptiness; however, it actually means the complete interdependence of all things. With this image Dōgen recalls the poem "Windbell" by his teacher, Tendō Nyojō:

The whole body of a windbell, like a mouth hanging
in emptiness (sunyata),
Without choosing which direction the wind
comes from,
For the sake of others equally speaks
prajna (wisdom). . . . [our translation]

24. This is a quotation from the Lotus Sutra, when the followers of Buddha who were not ready to hear the Mahayana teaching departed.

25. The seven buddhas are the incarnate buddhas dating back to previous eons, of whom Shakyamuni is considered the seventh.

26. The Hokke (Lotus) Sutra is the primary text of the Tendai School, and the Kegon (Flower Ornament) Sutra is the primary text of the Kegon School, two of the main Buddhist schools in Japan during Dōgen's time.

27. The Shingon (True Mantra) School, the other main Japanese Buddhist school at this time, is based on the Dainichi or Mahavairocana Sutra, in which the cosmic buddha Vairocana transmits this teaching to the bodhisattva Vajrasattva. This is the Japanese Vajrayana (Tantric) school.

28. The five buddhas are those depicted in the mandalas used in Shingon practice, at the four directions, and at the center. A *kalpa* is a vast duration of time.

29. An arhat is one who has attained the highest fruit of practice in Theravada Buddhism, which is the enlightenment after wiping away all defilements. Arhats are literally known as worthy of receiving offerings.

30. The twelvefold chain of causation is the early Buddhist teaching about the twelve-step process in the circular causal nexus of life and death, that is, samsara.

    The twenty-five realms of existence are categories from the Mahayana Mahaparinirvana Sutra.

    The three vehicles are shravakas (those who listen

to the teaching), pratyeka buddhas (self-enlightened ones), and bodhisattvas. There are also five vehicles systems, which include the three vehicles as well as humans, divine beings, and buddhas in different combinations.

31. Dōgen does not mean that Buddhist teachings must never be studied, but that they must actually be put into practice as well as studied.

32. "Great awakening" here is literally great bodhi, the enlightenment that goes beyond the distinction between delusion and enlightenment.

33. The three studies are precepts (*shila*), concentration (*samadhi*), and wisdom (*prajna*). The six perfections (*paramita*) are generosity (*dana*), ethical conduct or precepts (*shila*), patience or tolerance (*kshanti*), effort or diligence (*virya*), meditation (*dhyana*), and wisdom or insight (*prajna*).

34. True dharma eye treasury is *Shōbōgenzō*, the name of Dōgen's master work.

35. Shōrinji temple on Su Mountain is, in Chinese, Shaolin temple on Song Mountain. "Essence" is a translation of *shu* (宗), which also is the word for school in "Zen School."

36. "Worldly people" refers to those blindly enmeshed in worldly pursuits.

37. "The true dharma eye treasury of the wondrous mind of nirvana" is *Shōbōgenzō nehanmyoshin* (正法眼蔵涅槃妙心).

38. Nagarjuna (second–third century C.E.) was an early Mahayana teacher who elaborated the teaching of Emptiness (*sunyata*). He is considered one of the ancestors in the Zen lineage. In *Shōbōgenzō Zanmai Ō Zanmai* (The samadhi of the king of samadhis), Dōgen further discusses sitting posture.

39. The character for enlightenment here is *shō* (証), which also means verification, proof, or authentication. This character is used for enlightenment throughout Dōgen's reply.

40. This refers to a dialogue between the Sixth Ancestor and Nangaku (see note 12). The Sixth Ancestor asked, "What is this that thus comes?" After eight years Nangaku was able to answer, "Any explanation misses it." The Sixth Ancestor asked, "If so, is there practice and enlightenment?" Nangaku responded, "It is not that there is no practice and enlightenment, but only that they cannot be defiled." The Sixth Ancestor agreed, saying, "It is just this nondefilement that all buddha ancestors maintain."

41. A statement by Shikū Honjō (667–761, Sikong Benjing in Chinese), another disciple of the Sixth Ancestor.

42. Senika was an Indian philosopher contemporary with Shakyamuni Buddha.

43. Nanyō Echū (d. 775, Nanyuan Huizhong in Chinese) was a disciple of the Sixth Ancestor.

44. "Gate" refers to dharma gates or entryways into reality.

45. "Aspect" or "appearance" is *sō* (相), which is contrasted with "essence," *shō* (性), also translated sometimes as a thing's "nature." Dōgen here is referring to the *Awakening of Faith* which says, "The Mind in terms of the Absolute is the one World of Reality (dharma-dhatu) and the essence of all phases of existence in their totality. That which is called the 'essential nature of the Mind' is unborn and imperishable" (Yoshito Hakeda, *The Awakening of Faith Attributed to Asvaghosha* [New York: Columbia University Press, 1967], 32). Dōgen's comment is that the mind nature or essence is inseparable from its appearance or aspects as manifested.

46. "Sacred practice" is *bongyō* (梵行). *Gyō* means practice. *Bon* is a transliteration for Brahma, the Indian deity. *Bongyō* is used for *brahmacarya*, the practice of cutting off all defiled desires.

47. *Shingon* and *shikan* were the two traditional practices in Japan before Dōgen. Shingon is the esoteric or mantrayana practice of the Shingon School (see note 27). *Shikan* is the translation for *shamatha-vipasyana*

(stopping or concentration; and insight). This was the traditional meditation developed in the Tendai School, the denomination at Mount Hiei where Dōgen was ordained. The Tendai School of Dōgen's time also strongly included esoteric practice.

48. Unmon Bun'en (864–949, Yunmen Wenyan in Chinese) said, "If you don't rely on one thing, you will not develop one wisdom." Yunmen was founder of one of the five classic houses of Chinese Zen and was noted for his pithy comments on the dharma.

49. Daisō (r. 762–779, in Chinese Daizong) and Junso (r. 805, in Chinese Shunzong) were Tang Dynasty emperors.

50. Prime Minister Ri (d. 844, Li in Chinese) was a student of Yakusan Igen (Yaoshan Weiyen in Chinese). Prime Minister Bo (Fang in Chinese) may have been a student of Ōbaku Kiun (Huangbo Xiyun in Chinese), teacher of Rinzai.

51. Hyoshu (d. 1153, Fengji in Chinese) studied with Daie Soko (1085–1163, Dahui Zongkao in Chinese).

52. "Worst criminals" refers to those who commit the five most evil deeds: killing one's mother, killing one's father, killing an arhat (saint), shedding the blood of a buddha, and creating disorder in the sangha. For example, King Ajatasatru, who caused the death of his father King Bimbisara, was later an enlightened patron of the Buddhist order. Examples of hunters and woodcutters are Sekkyō Ezō (Shigong Huican in Chinese), a hunter who became a disciple of the great Baso (Mazu); and Daikan Enō (Huineng), the woodcutter who became the Sixth Ancestor.

53. The "corrupt declining age" refers to the Buddhist theory of three ages of dharma: the True Dharma when the teaching, practice, and enlightenment are all present; the Semblance Dharma when only teaching and practice exist; and the Final Dharma (*mappō*) when only the

teaching remains. The belief that the final degenerate age had arrived was widespread and influential in Dōgen's time, although he rejected it.

54. Hō'on Gensoku (ninth–tenth century; Baoen Xuanze in Chinese) later became a dharma heir of Hōgen Mon'eki (885–958, Fayan Wenyi in Chinese), considered the founder of the Fayan School. The director is a monastery's head administrator.

55. Seihō is not known with certainty, but this may refer to Hakuchō Shien (ninth century, Baizhao Zhiyuan in Chinese).

56. "Fire Boy" is *heiteidōji* (丙丁童字), which also could be read "fire-spirit's apprentice," referring to fire as one of the five elements in Chinese cosmology. The heiteidōji was the novice in the monastery who attended to the lamps.

57. Hōgen's response emphasizes the necessity of the actual "seeking" of the self for the self.

58. This question refers to four enlightenment stories. Kyogen Chikan (d. 898, Xiangyan Zhixian in Chinese), a student of Isan (Guishan), awakened while sweeping when he heard a pebble strike bamboo. Reiun Shigon (ninth century, Lingyun Zhiqin in Chinese) another student of Isan, awakened seeing peach blossoms. Ananda, Shakyamuni's attendant and disciple, later asked Mahakashyapa, "What did the Buddha transmit to you besides his robe?" Mahakashyapa said, "Ananda!" Ananda said, "Yes?" Mahakashyapa said, "Take down the banner pole in front of the gate." Ananda awakened. For Reiun's story see Robert Aitken, trans., *The Gateless Barrier*: The Wu–men Kuan (*Mumonkan*) (San Francisco: North Point Press, 1990), Case 16. For Ananda's story see Thomas Cleary, trans., *Transmission of Light: Zen in the Art of Enlightenment* by Zen Master Keizan (San Francisco: North Point Press, 1990), p. 10.

59. This refers to stories about two of Shakyamuni's enlightened disciples. An old man who could not comprehend the simplest of teachings was teased by a mischievous young monk who told him he could become enlightened by being hit by a ball. Because of the old man's deep though simple faith, the first time he was struck by a hurled ball, he entered the first stage (in the Theravada system) of stream-winner; the second time the stage of once-returner; the third time the stage of never-returner; and the fourth time he was struck he became a full-fledged arhat.

    The second story refers to a woman who in a past life was a prostitute and put on an *okesa* (priest robe) as a joke. The merit from this act, even done in jest, allowed her to become a nun in the next rebirth, and later she was a nun who became an arhat under Shakyamuni's guidance.

60. In Buddhism, faith is not belief in some external doctrine or deity, but trusting and acting in one's experience and realization of dharma truth.

61. This story is from the *Zōbōkyo* (Miscellaneous sutra treasury), part of the Theravada Agama group of sutras. After offering the monk a meal, the devout woman closed her eyes waiting for the customary dharma talk after an offering. The monk could think of nothing and fled, but the woman, thanks to her faith, was awakened. She found the monk and thanked him, upon which he, too, was enlightened.

62. This "three thousand worlds" is an abbreviation for three thousand great thousand worlds, or one thousand to the third power, meaning one billion worlds. This is the realm of one buddha.

63. The Japanese Emperor Kinmei reigned from 540 to 571. Emperor Yōmei reigned from 586 to 588 and was father of Prince Shōtoku, the revered early patron of Buddhism in Japan.

64. Ryūge Koton (835–923, Longya Judun in Chinese) was a

dharma heir of Tōzan Ryokai (807–869, Dongshan Liangjie in Chinese), the founder of the Sōtō lineage in China. Dōgen quotes Ryūge in *Shōbōgenzō Zuimonki*, 4–14: "To study the Way, first of all, you must learn poverty. After having learned poverty and become poor, you will be intimate with the Way." From Shohaku Okumura, trans. *Shōbōgenzō Zuimonki* (Kyoto: Kyoto Sōtō Zen Center, 1987), p. 162.

Kukkutupada (Keisoku in Japanese) is the mountain in central India where Mahakashyapa practiced and died—or, it is sometimes said, where he is still waiting to pass on Shakyamuni's robe to Maitreya, the future buddha. Mahakashyapa was considered foremost among Shakyamuni's disciples in ascetic practice. *Ryūge* is literally "dragon tusk" and *Kukkutupada* means "chicken foot."

65. *Fukanzazengi* (The form for universally recommended zazen) was written by Dōgen in 1227 when he returned from China in order to convey the true meaning and procedure for zazen.

66. The "mid-autumn day" is the full moon day of the second month of autumn, the fifteenth day of the eighth lunar month. *Shamon* comes from the Sanskrit word *shramana*, which means a mendicant practitioner or monk.

Commentary on Bendōwa
by Uchiyama Roshi

Part One

THAT WHICH CANNOT BE TRANSMITTED, THE SELF THAT IS ONLY THE
SELF, IS TRANSMITTED THROUGH ZAZEN. THAT IS WHY ZAZEN IS
CALLED THE MARVELOUS DHARMA.

Usually we begin to practice the buddha way
with an idea that practice has no meaning
unless we attain enlightenment and become great persons.
However, this is completely contrary to the true buddha
way. We must see the difference between this kind of
worldly idea and the real buddha way. Then we must put all
of our energy into practicing it. This is the meaning of *ben*
in *Bendōwa*.

What is the true buddha way? It is jijuyu zanmai. I will
explain this in relation to the next part of the text.

*All buddha-tathagatas together have been simply transmit-
ting wondrous dharma and actualizing anuttara samyak sambodhi for which there is an unsurpassable, unfabricated, wondrous
method.*

Whenever I encounter the word *buddha* in a text, I am
not satisfied unless I talk about what its real meaning is.
However, I'll pass it by for now and go on to the next
phrase, "wondrous dharma" (*myōhō*), because it is more trou-
blesome.

Among all the chapters considered part of *Shōbōgenzō* in the later *Honzan* version, I think *Bendōwa* and *Genjōkōan* are the most popular. The other chapters seem rather difficult to understand, but *Bendōwa* and *Genjōkōan* are relatively easy, and I think this is why many people like to read them.

However, you will probably find that you do not really understand them even after a number of readings. They seem understandable, but it is not easy to grasp their true meaning. Various renditions into modern Japanese, as well as commentaries, have been published recently. Even if you read all of them, you would not understand what Dōgen really meant. Why is that so? It is only natural. No commentary or record of *teishō* on these two chapters explains dharma or, in this case, "wondrous dharma." I have never found any that render this term into modern Japanese. Furthermore, in the opening paragraph of *Genjōkōan* we find expressions such as *shohō* or *banpō*, both of which imply myriad dharmas. Neither of these terms is explained in any commentary. Some commentaries on *Bendōwa* simply say that dharma means buddha-dharma. They deal with these technical terms only by using other technical terms.

Since there are no explanations of dharma, which is the most important word in the text, no one will understand it. Needless to say, dharma cannot be grasped with the intellect. But if it is completely incomprehensible, we should not bother to talk about it at all. We have to understand, at least intellectually, why buddha-dharma cannot be grasped with the intellect. Otherwise it becomes complete nonsense. So what on earth does dharma mean here? Instead of simply saying "Words cannot explain it" or "The buddha-dharma is precious," we have to start by making a thorough investigation of dharma as a matter closely related to ourselves.

First of all, in the *Abhidharma Kosha*, it is said that a dharma is something that keeps its own nature and does not change. It becomes a code for recognizing things. For example, here is a cup, and this cup seems to have its own nature. This was a cup yesterday, and it is still a cup today. It seems as if its self nature doesn't change. Yet actually everything is changing. This cup will not be a cup if it falls on the floor and breaks. It does not keep its self nature.

The *Abhidharma Kosha* was written in terms of the philosophy of an Indian Buddhist school called Sarvastivadin. [This name refers to those who insist that all dharmas exist and are real.] One of the basic theories in the *Abhidharma Kosha* is that each phenomenal and individual thing is empty, but that dharmas exist and are real. This is similar to an idea in Greek philosophy that the past, present, and future actually exist and entities exist eternally. The Sarvastivadins thought that each phenomenal thing is not substantial, but dharmas and elemental entities are substantial. According to this philosophy, this cup does not exist as a substance, yet it remains in existence as an entity. This is called material dharma (*shikihō* or *rupa dharma*), and the Sarvastivadins thought everything exists in this way.

They called the objects of our senses and consciousness dharmas as objects (*hōshō* or *hōkyō*). This means that when our senses and consciousness encounter something outside of ourselves, we recognize that it exists. This is why they called everything we encounter the myriad dharmas (*shōhō* or *banpō*). Dharma, in this sense, means all existence. They also used the word *dharma*, as in buddha-dharma, to mean the Buddha's teachings (in the sense of the reality or truth of the myriad dharmas), and to mean the method we must follow in doing something. In this third interpretation *dharma* also means rules, regulations, morals, customs, and laws.

I have given a brief explanation of the various meanings of dharma according to the *Abhidharma*, but what I want to say next is much more important. In Mahayana Buddhism, and especially in Dōgen Zenji's teachings, the meaning of dharma has more depth. According to the concepts we accept, we think that everything exists as objects outside the self. For example, we usually think that all phenomenal things that appear before our eyes, or this twentieth-century human society, have existence outside our individual self. We believe that when we are born we appear on this world's stage, and when we die we leave that stage. All of us think this way. But the truth is that this common-sense concept is questionable.

Mahayana Buddhism began from a reexamination of this common-sense attitude. I'll give you one of my favorite examples. I am looking at this cup now. You are also looking at the same cup. We think that we are looking at the very same cup, but this is not true. I am looking at it from my angle, with my eyesight, in the lighting that occurs where I am sitting, and with my own feelings or emotions. Furthermore, the angle, my feeling, and everything else is changing from moment to moment. This cup I am looking at now is not the same one that I will be looking at in the next moment. Each of you is also looking at it from your own angle, with your eyesight, with your own feelings, and these also are constantly changing.

This is the way actual life experience is. However, if we use our common-sense way of thinking, we think we are looking at the very same cup. This is an abstraction and not the reality of life. Abstract concepts and living reality are entirely different. The Buddhist view is completely different from our ordinary thinking.

Western philosophy's way of thinking is also based on abstractions. It assumes that all of us are seeing the same cup. Greek philosophers went further and further in their abstractions until they came up with the concept of the idea that cannot be seen or felt. One example is Venus, the goddess of beauty. In the real world, no woman is as well-proportioned as Venus, or embodies perfect beauty as she does. Yet the Greeks idealized beauty and created a statue of Venus, just as they had thought of the "idea" of a circle that is abstracted from something round. In other words, the Greek way of thinking is abstraction to the highest degree. Buddhism is different. Buddhism puts emphasis on life, the actual life experience of the reality of the self.

In mathematics, one plus one equals two. None of us doubt this. But actually, this is only correct from the standpoint of mathematics. In life experience, when my car crashes into another car, the hoods are dented, tires come off, and glass breaks into pieces. No cars remain. With cars, one plus one makes zero, or we could say that one plus one makes infinity, because the two cars break apart into an infinite number of pieces.

The following example is even clearer. One man plus one woman makes three or four when they have children.

Once I took a piss in the ocean. At that moment I clearly understood that one plus one makes only one. The one was the ocean. Nothing was changed even after my piss was added. The ocean was not concerned about my piss at all.

What Buddhism is concerned about is not something abstract, but the very concrete and actual reality of life. All beings exist through life experience of the self. The self lives out itself in the life experience of all beings. The life experience of the self and the myriad beings that we experience are one. This is the reality of life. The life experience of the self and the life experience of all beings can never separate into subject and object. That which experiences and that which is experienced cannot be divided into two. This reality that cannot be differentiated into two is called dharma or mind, and it is the meaning of the expression "dharma and mind are one reality" (*shinpō ichinyo*).

Therefore, we cannot say that we appear on the world's stage when we are born, and leave it when we die. We were born with this world in which we live out our lives as life experience. We live with this whole world. When we die, our whole world will die with us also. If you interpret this incorrectly, it might be mistaken for experiential idealism [the idea of experience as produced by our consciousness]. This philosophy is the basis of *Seichō no ie*, one of the new Japanese religions. Yet what I am talking about is totally different.

People involved in *Seichō no ie* think that material existence is the shadow of our mind. They say that if we think there is no sickness, it won't exist. Then what will happen if a dump truck is coming toward you? If you think that the truck is a shadow of your mind, will the truck disappear? If you are lucky, the truck driver will yell, "You idiot! Where are your eyes?" If you are not lucky, you will be run over and killed. This is reality. What I am talking about is not experiential idealism. We recognize things through abstractions in our mind or consciousness, but those conceptualized things are not the reality of life. If we say the word *fire*, our tongues will not be burned. The force that is reflecting, imagining, abstracting, and conceptualizing things is the reality of life.

The reality of life for human beings who have rational faculties includes reason. If we cut off the rational faculty, there is no reality of human life. This is the point at which the reality of life is entirely different from the theory that material existence is only a shadow of the mind.

The reality of life has a multidimensional structure, and since it has many aspects, it is very difficult to explain in words. Yet the reality of life experience is just one and can never be divided. It is not two.

Dōgen Zenji expressed this nondualistic reality in *Shōbōgenzō Sokushin Zebutsu* (Mind is itself buddha) in the following way: "The mind which has been properly transmitted is one mind that is myriad dharmas, and myriad dharmas are one mind." People today think that mind means the functioning of psychological consciousness. However, if you think this way you won't be able to understand Buddhism. When the word *mind* is used in Buddhist texts, it often means the vivid life experience that I have been talking about. This is what the word *mind* means when Dōgen talks about that which has been correctly transmitted in Buddhism. "One mind is myriad dharmas" means that the one mind includes the myriad dharmas, or my life experience of the world. This is the meaning of mind and dharma in Buddhism.

In *Shōbōgenzō Beppon Butsukōjōji* (Another version of the matter going beyond buddha) we find, "Buddha-dharma is the myriad dharmas, the hundred grasses." Buddha-dharma is all myriad dharmas, which is the reality that includes my own life experience. I was born. I am living. I am going to die. This is the life of a buddha. Dōgen Zenji also said in *Shōbōgenzō Shōji* (Life and death) that life and death is the life of buddha. After all, for each and every one of us, being born, living, and dying is the complete expression of our life experience. Nothing is more precious than this life experience of the self. The only basis of any possible system of values must be the fact that I am living right now, right here. This vitality of buddha has the highest value.

Therefore, a lowbrow idea such as that money is most important is below criticism. It is possible for you to think that money is important or that social status is desirable only because you are alive. Someone said that the emperor is the most important person in this country, but he has this opinion only because he lives in Japan as a Japanese. If he were born in America as an American, there would be no reason to place such importance on the Japanese emperor.

Something that can be evaluated in various ways depending upon arbitrary conditions is not really valuable. The most valuable thing is the fact that we are living right here and now, and this must be the basis of all evaluation. This life experience is the foundation of all existence and the basis of the world, so for this reason we call it buddha-dharma and give it absolute value.

When we hear the word *buddha*, we usually think of the buddha statues in the main hall of a temple, but those are just dolls. The real buddha is nothing but the zazen we practice. The buddha statues enshrined in temples are no more than models of zazen. When you clearly understand this, you should then think once more about the expression, "all buddha-tathagatas together have been simply transmitting wondrous dharma." What does this mean?

When people hear "transmitting wondrous dharma," they are apt to think that the wondrous dharma is something like a scroll on which some kind of hidden mystery is written. They imagine that this dharma scroll is transmitted from one person to another secretly, and when one receives it that person becomes great. Yet this has nothing to do with what Dōgen Zenji meant by transmitting wondrous dharma. In essence, "one mind is the myriad dharmas, and myriad dharmas are the one mind" means that the absolute self is the life experience of the self. Therefore, it is impossible to transmit it from one person to another. As Sawaki Roshi used to say, we cannot exchange so much as a fart with another person. This is the nature of the real self.

In spite of the fact that it cannot be transmitted, it is somehow transmitted. It is called wondrous because the dharma that cannot be transmitted in fact has been transmitted right up to this moment, and is present right now.

Therefore, when we read *Bendōwa*, the most important thing for us to do is to understand wondrous dharma in this way. If you read *Bendōwa* after you have understood what dharma is, then you might understand the essence of what Dōgen Zenji taught. If you don't understand what dharma is, you won't be able to grasp the true meaning no matter how many times you read *Bendōwa* or commentaries on it.

"All buddha-tathagatas have been actualizing anuttara samyaku sambodhi." *Anuttara samyaku sambodhi* is a Sanskrit phrase that is rendered into Japanese as *mujō shōtō kaku* (the ultimate right awareness). *Mujō* (ultimate) means "incomparable or absolute," and *shō* (right) means "to be one." There is only one absolute reality. It is prior to any division, in other words, not two. There will be only one reality forever. *Jitsubutsu* (reality) is my term for that, and it means "being alive." *Tō* (equality) in *shoto* means "all beings are equal and are without differentiation." Usually we think that this thing and that thing are different, but their foundation is the reality of our life experience, the reality before division. However, even though there is just one reality of life experience, we human beings differentiate things and say, "This is a pine tree," or "This is a wall." Such discrimination is simply the scenery of life. Having clear vision of this one reality is called *kaku* (awakening).

In the *Honyaku myōgishu* [a text explaining translated Buddhist terms], it is said that this means awakening from the dream of samsara (life and death). There is a famous verse, "Today, crossing the deep mountains of human fabrication, I am beyond dreaming and intoxication." Waking up from the dream of samsara is called *kaku*. Fabrication means basing one's life on notions created in the human mind. Lack of fabrication means living out the reality of life as it is, without relying on anything created in the human mind. This is the ultimate way of life, yet it can never be expressed in words, and so it is called wondrous.

There is an unsurpassable, unfabricated, wondrous method. This wondrous dharma, which has been transmitted only from buddha to buddha without deviation, has as its criterion jijuyu zanmai.

Dharma is the reality of life, and each and every one of us is living out absolute life, no matter what situation we find ourselves in. We live out the self that is only the self. No one can become a different person. In a sense, from birth to death, we are completely alone. Even if you think that you have good friends, family, or a loving wife, the fact is that your wife can never be you. You and your wife have different dreams and think differently. We sometimes say that we know everything about an intimate friend, but that is really just something that we have thought up. It is impossible to really understand another person. In this sense, every one of us is living out the self that is only the self, and living out the present that is only the present. This is an absolute truth.

These days, probably as a result of the development of bulldozers and other power equipment, archaeologists dig here and there excavating ancient artifacts like pottery and swords. They claim that some were made a thousand years ago or ten thousand years ago, but there is no absolute way to exactly prove this (aside from our present views). Buddhist scholars argue whether Shakyamuni Buddha was born in the fourth or fifth century B.C.E. It is impossible to prove this too. [According to the viewpoints of historians,] it may not even be clear that Shakyamuni Buddha ever lived. Everything in the past is uncertain.

In other words, time itself is uncertain. We say that this temple is quite old, but this only means that we imagine the past through what it looks like at this present moment. Other people are nothing but myself, and the past is nothing but the present. No one thinks this temple was built recently. It obviously looks old in the present, but these sliding doors look new in the present.

As we can see from this example, whether something is old or new is simply the nature of reality as we are encountering it, at this moment. From the nature of reality in our life experience at the present time, we say these sliding doors are new, or the ceiling is old. We imagine that this ceiling was made several decades or several centuries ago because of its present nature of appearing old. Yet in reality, only the present exists. The past and the future do not exist [separate from the present].

Each and every one of us, without exception, is living out the self which is only the self and the present that is only the present. This is the reality of life regardless of whether we think it is true or not.

Yet in spite of this, we usually think that things existed in the past or that there are things outside of our self. As long as we think this way, we remain separated from reality in an illusion produced in our minds. Actually, each one of us is living out the self that is exactly the self, and living out the present that is exactly the present.

This is what *jijuyu zanmai* means. Sawaki Roshi, my

late teacher, used to express *jijuyu zanmai* as "the self making the self into the self." This jijuyu zanmai is the foundation of the reality of life experience, and for this reason it is said that the criterion of dharma is jijuyu zanmai.

For disporting oneself freely in this samadhi, practicing zazen in an upright posture is the true gate.

Practicing zazen is the true gate to playing in this samadhi of the self that is only the self. The other side of this statement is that only practicing the zazen of the absolute self and absolute present is jijuyu zanmai. Yet if you assume the zazen posture and think that satori or buddha is outside of yourself, it will not be possible to enter jijuyu zanmai.

Although this dharma is abundantly inherent in each person, it is not manifested without practice; it is not attained without realization.

This self that is only the self, the vivid reality of life, is abundantly inherent in all people. There is no one who lacks it. You cannot fail or succeed in practicing zazen. This truth is obvious. No one can do anything but live out the self. However, in some prescribed paths of practice it is necessary to receive the affirmation of your teacher after having practiced a certain length of time. If your teacher says your realization is correct, you succeed. If not, you fail. Even though many people try with all their might, I would guess that the percentage of people who gain satori is low. The gate to enlightenment for them must be narrower than the gate to Japanese universities is for Japanese students.

However, the zazen taught by Dōgen Zenji is not like that; it is zazen as a true religion. It is not zazen as a kind of discipline or training. There is no failure or success in zazen as a true religion. All of us can be saved. This is only natural because we just practice the reality of life that is abundantly inherent in every person.

However, the reality of life is not manifested without practicing zazen, and it is actualized only inasmuch as you practice zazen. The reality of life is not attained without realization. If you do not actualize the reality of life, it is not attained.

When you let go, the dharma fills your hands; it is not within the boundary of one or many. When you try to speak, it fills your mouth, it is not limited to vertical or horizontal.

When we practice this zazen that actualizes the reality of life, we become the universal self only when we let go of illusory thoughts that stray from reality. My expression for "letting go" is "opening the hand of thought." When we open the hand of thought, the dharma fills our hands; the universal reality of life is right here. This reality of life fills your mouth when you speak. It cannot be limited vertically or horizontally, and it can be expressed in immeasurable ways.

Buddhas constantly dwell in and maintain this dharma, yet no trace of conceptualization remains.

All Buddhas are dwelling in and maintaining this jijuyū zanmai. However, although they are dwelling in and maintaining it, they never perceive samadhi; this consciousness does not exist.

It is the same as driving a car. When you drive a car, pedestrians and cars coming from the opposite direction are reflected in your vision. You turn the steering wheel to the right or left, and step on the brake or gas pedal, performing these actions without being conscious of them. You drive a car just as if you are moving your own body. When you can drive that way, you drive freely. There is no trace of conception. We drive freely in jijuyu zanmai.

Living beings constantly function in and use this dharma, yet it does not appear in their perception.

We living beings have been living out the self that is only the self and the life that is only life from the beginning, yet no aspect appears in our perception. In our day-to-day activities we fail to freely drive ourselves.

The wholehearted practice of the Way that I am talking about allows all things to exist in enlightenment and enables us to live out oneness in the path of emancipation. When we break through the barrier and drop off all limitations, we are no longer concerned with conceptional distinctions.

"Enlightenment" is the reality of life; "all things" means all the different kinds of scenery in our life. So the practice of the way that we are talking about enables all different kinds of situations in our life to exist in awareness of the reality of life. The path of emancipation means actualizing indivisible life (one absolute reality) without being deterred by any "other."

"Breaking through the barrier and dropping off limitations" means that we usually build a barrier between ourselves and the outside world. We separate ourselves and others, subject and object. When we go beyond this barrier by letting go of thoughts, then all conceptional distinctions and verbal explanations like the ones I have been giving are no longer necessary.

Being Enlightened Is Putting Your Feet on the Ground of the Reality of Life

After Dōgen aroused bodhi mind and aspired to seek buddha-dharma, he visited various teachers in Japan. Among these teachers, he studied and practiced the way of Rinzai Zen for nine years with master Myōzen, who was the senior disciple of the famous Zen master Eisai. Later Myōzen went to China with Dōgen Zenji and died there. Myōzen must have been a great person. Dōgen Zenji praised him any time he could. Here, too, he praises Myōzen saying that "Master Myōzen was a great disciple of Zen Master Eisai, from whom he alone received correct transmission of the unsurpassable buddha-dharma," and that he had no equal.

Later I went to Song China and visited various masters in Zhejiang Province, where I learned the ways of the five schools of Zen.

Dōgen Zenji himself was not satisfied with his practice in Japan and went to Song China with his master. They visited various masters in the province of Zhejiang, and Dōgen Zenji learned the ways of the five schools of Zen. The Qiantong River, which flows from west to east, divides the province into north and south. That is why Dōgen Zenji said he "visited teachers in both parts of Zhejiang province." At that time Zen Buddhism was in full bloom in China, and this area was the center of Zen Buddhism. Dōgen Zenji travelled about visiting various masters and studying the ways of the five schools of Zen: Hōgen, Igyō, Unmon, Rinzai, and Sōtō.

However, he was dissatisfied with what he saw, and decided to go back to Japan. On his way back he heard of Zen master Nyojō, who had just become the abbot of a monastery Dōgen Zenji had once stayed at on Mount Tendo (Tiantong in Chinese). Dōgen Zenji visited Nyojō, decided to practice under him, and finally completely clarified the Way of practice throughout this lifetime. He gained the buddha way.

When you hear "completely clarified the great matter of lifelong practice," you probably think this means you don't have to practice anymore, but it is not true. Completing life's great matter, gaining the Way, or attaining satori means only that you have clarified the true meaning of practice, clearly understand in which direction you have to go, and on what you should place absolute value in life.

We usually live our lives without a sense of the true point. All of us become prisoners of our own desires and wander here and there without any direction. "Clarifying the Way" means that we determine the point we should aim at throughout our lives, based on the self that is only the self and life that is only life. This is the sole great matter, and this is what "completing the sole great matter of one's life" means. True practice begins at this point.

[After he realized the buddha way] Dōgen Zenji returned to Japan. Spreading this dharma and saving all living beings had become his vow. This vow is most important for Buddhist practitioners.

However, spreading the dharma and saving all living beings is not an easy thing to do in this day and age. We also can't help feeling that we are carrying a heavy burden on our shoulders.

A contemporary way is to try to become famous through the mass media, lecture all over the country, or write and sell a lot of books. But the buddha-dharma is different from a commercially advertised product. If you really understand the self that is only the self and life that is only life, you don't propagate it like this.

Some Buddhist bluffers are going to America or Europe and collecting money. It appears that there are some millionaires who are willing to give them huge donations. These Buddhist bluffers then build imposing temples and try to get people to come to them.

The zazen practiced among the followers of Bodhidharma and Dōgen Zenji has nothing to do with whether we have a magnificent building or not. What's really important is to foster real practitioners. To do that we have to teach bit by bit. The followers of Bodhidharma must persist in this way no matter where they go.

In my case, when I was practicing under Sawaki Roshi, since he used to travel from one place to another to teach, I usually sat *sesshin* [all-day zazen, often for five or seven days] by myself without speaking to anyone. When Sawaki Roshi came back I sat with him and with others who came. I continued this way of practice without fellow practitioners from the time I became a monk in 1941 until around 1955. In 1957 Satō Myōshin joined me, and around 1960 Honda Tekifu came. Watanabe Kōhō, who later took over Antaiji, came in 1962. After that the number of people who sat with me gradually began to increase, and after a while dozens of people began to gather for sesshin at Antaiji.

Before doing anything else, first determine your aim and sit alone. This is like sowing seeds. The seeds germinate when spring comes. However, during the cold winter, plants can only spread their roots little by little. If plants do not take deep enough root, they won't grow after they sprout. As for fostering practitioners, we should not think in terms of five or ten years. I think in terms of several centuries. We have to increase the number of people who really devote themselves to the practice of Dōgen Zenji's zazen one by one. In this sense the spring has not yet come; now is the winter when zazen has just begun to take root.

This is what Dōgen Zenji meant when he said,

In spite of that, I set aside my vow to propagate this, in order to wait for conditions under which it could flourish. For now I will live alone, moving from place to place like a cloud or duckweed, and follow the way of the ancient sages.

While he was writing *Bendōwa* Dōgen Zenji was moving from one place to another. This was in 1231, when he was 32 years old. Dōgen Zenji came back from China in 1228 and first stayed at Kenninji temple in Kyoto, where he had practiced before he went to China. However, two years later he had to move into Anyoin temple in Fukakusa, outside Kyoto, because of oppression from the Tendai school at Mount Hiei.

The way of the ancient sages means the way of life of one who does not have a certain place to settle down, and moves from one place to another. Bodhidharma, the First Ancestor of China, came to China from India and after wandering here and there, he entered Mount Shaolin and became a parasite at a monastery of the Ritsu (Precept) School. He did not take up his own abode. This is the lifestyle of a cloud or a water plant.

However, there might be some sincere practitioners who on their own do not seek after fame or profit, and who give priority to the mind that seeks the Way.

Since he lived like this, even if there were some sincere practitioners who weren't concerned with gaining fame or profit and had true aspiration to seek the Way, they would not be able to find the Way through him.

When we read the collections of biographies of famous priests, we find that almost all the priests who were regarded as famous or venerable people at that time were patronized by emperors or aristocrats and given access to the imperial palace. They attended the empress or the imperial concubines when they were ill, and offered prayers for their recovery. In return they received favored status or were presented beautiful robes. They sought after fame and profit and made light of bodhi mind. They were all false practitioners. If no one had shown the true buddha way, all monks would have been subordinate to those priests, even if some of the monks had true aspiration to begin with. It would have been the inevitable result.

They still may be vainly led astray by false teachers, and recklessly cover up correct understanding and become drunk in their own confusion, sinking into delusion for a long time. How will it be possible for [these sincere practitioners] to nurture the true seed of prajna and have appropriate occasion to attain the Way?

Therefore, Dōgen Zenji was carried away by the feeling that,

Since this unworthy wayfarer [Dōgen] is now living like a cloud or duckweed, how will they find the mountain or river where they can visit me?

For this reason,

Because I care about these people, I have collected and written about what I saw with my own eyes of the style of practice in the Zen monasteries of Song China, and what I received and uphold as the profound teaching of my master, and I leave this for devoted practitioners of the way of serenity in order to let them know about the true dharma of buddhas. Here is the genuine expression of the essence.

He wrote down what he heard and saw in Chinese monasteries regarding true practice of zazen and the true buddha-dharma taught by Nyojō Zenji. The buddha way manifested as concrete everyday activities. He left these words so that sincere practitioners of the Way might understand the true dharma of the Buddha.

Great Teacher Shakyamuni Buddha imparted the dharma to

Mahakashyapa at the Vulture Peak assembly, and it was correctly transmitted from ancestor to ancestor until it reached the venerable Bodhidharma. Bodhidharma himself went to China and imparted the dharma to the Great Teacher Eka. This was the first transmission of the buddha-dharma in the East (China).

Here we trace the dharma back to Shakyamuni Buddha.

There is a story about Shakyamuni and Mahakashyapa. In front of a great assembly, Shakyamuni picked up a flower and twirled it a little. No one could understand the meaning, and they kept silent. Only venerable Mahakashyapa smiled. It is said that the Buddha's true dharma was transmitted to venerable Mahakashyapa at that time.

After that the dharma was transmitted through various ancestors generation to generation, and finally venerable Bodhidharma received the dharma as the Twenty-eighth Ancestor. The great master Bodhidharma went to China and transmitted the dharma to the great master Eka. That was the first transmission of dharma from India to the East.

At that time, the authentic buddha-dharma actually spread throughout China, and reality beyond conceptual distinctions was manifested.

Buddhist scriptures were first introduced into China in the latter Han dynasty (first century B.C.E.) However, even though concepts were imported through scriptures and teachings were studied through words, it was not real. It was stiff and awkward.

The living human being who embodies enlightenment and who is a real example of buddha-dharma would not be so uncouth. Buddha-dharma was unmistakenly transmitted from the great master Bodhidharma to the great master Eka, and it was handed down one to another, generation to generation, reaching the Sixth Ancestor Enō.

There were two superior disciples under the Sixth Ancestor, Seigen Gyoshi and Nangaku Ejo. Both of them held the buddha mudra and were equally teachers of all living beings. *Mudra* means "a mark or seal," which is zazen. In the streams of those two masters who transmitted and maintained zazen, five gates were later established: that is, Hogen, Igyō, Sōtō, Unmon, and Rinzai. By the time of Dōgen Zenj, only the Rinzai school was flourishing throughout Song China.

Each one of the five schools had its own characteristics, yet essentially they maintained only one buddha mind mudra. Each and every one of them equally actualized only one buddha teaching through the mind mudra, that is, zazen. Before these living examples, no one in China knew which was the real teaching of the Buddha. Buddhism as a religion has various aspects. We could say that every aspect in our lives is included in Buddhism. Among those miscellaneous elements, what is the true and basic thing? This question was not clearly answered. The great master Bodhidharma came to China and cut off the root of this complicated problem like cutting a wisteria vine. The essential point of Buddhism was revealed by showing a real, living example.

Therefore, Dōgen Zenji said,

We cannot help but yearn for this to happen in our country also.

For all ancestors and buddhas who have been dwelling in and maintaining buddha-dharma, practicing upright sitting in jijuyu zanmai is the true path for opening up enlightenment. Both in India and in China, those who have attained enlightenment have followed this way. This is because each teacher and each disciple has been intimately and correctly transmitting this subtle method and receiving and maintaining its true spirit.

In this part Dōgen Zenji reiterates what he said in the very beginning. "All buddha-tathagatas have been simply transmitting wondrous dharma and actualizing anuttara samyak sambodhi for which there is an unsurpassable, unfabricated, wondrous method. This wondrous dharma, which has been transmitted only from buddha to buddha without deviation, has as its criterion jijuyu zanmai." The buddha-dharma has been maintained by transmitting the buddha mudra of jijuyu zanmai, or sitting zazen. Above everything else, this is the point Dōgen Zenji is trying to make in *Bendōwa*.

Usually Dōgen Zenji directly states the most important thing in the very beginning of his writings and repeats it in the text for emphasis. This is also the case here. The vital point in *Bendōwa* is this jijuyu zanmai. Therefore I'd like to talk about it once again to emphasize its importance a little more. In the beginning of this talk I discussed "dharma" in detail. It is far different from what we think of as common sense in the ordinary world. You may think that you understand and accept it when you are listening to me talk about it, but after you go back to your day-to-day life, you get confused and gradually forget about it.

We should not listen to the buddha-dharma in a light way. We have to listen to the buddha-dharma in a way such that the dharma permeates into the core of our mind and becomes our bone and marrow, so that we won't forget it no matter what happens to us. This is the crucial point in *Bendōwa*. Unless we grasp this, we will never be able to understand *Bendōwa* as buddha-dharma.

Although we always think that we are really living, as a matter of fact we are not living out the reality of life. It is essential to become aware of this fact. Well then, in what way are we living? In a word, each and every one of us lives by treating abstract concepts as real.

We treat abstract concepts as if they are real and live in a world created by these abstract concepts. As I said before, we assume that each one of us sees the very same cup. But in reality, we do not see the same cup. Each person sees it from his own individual viewpoint.

The Japanese word for abstract is *chūshō*. *Chū* means to pull out, and *shō* means shape or form. We take the concept of a cup from real experience, and think there exists one cup that we are all looking at. This is treating abstract concepts as if they are real, and we should understand this clearly. Not only when we look at a cup, but throughout our lives we make the same mistake. For example, when we use the word *society*, we assume that we are living in the same society. But this is far from reality. Each person has his own picture of society which is different from anyone else's. Yet we take it for granted that all of us understand society in the same way. A great deviation from reality arises here. Each individual is living in his or her own particular society.

When I began to live by takuhatsu in 1949, people could not care less about five-sen or ten-sen bills. Yet for me, each of those bills was my lifeline. I rarely received ten-yen coins. So when I was given four ten-yen coins one after another, I could not help gloating. And if somebody gave me a one-hundred-yen bill, I lost my motivation, stopped doing takuhatsu for that day, and went back to the temple right away.

I have no idea of the purchasing power of money today, but I have often heard that a ten-thousand-yen bill disappears before you know it when you go shopping these days. I recently read a newspaper article about purse-snatching. A purse that contained her bonus—300,000 yen—was stolen from a young woman. What surprised me was that a young woman would receive such a large bonus. She must have felt it was a lot of money, but for me it was an inconceivable sum. On the other hand, there must be some rich people who could not care less about such a small amount of money.

Money is only one example of a subject for which there are innumerable viewpoints. If there are one hundred people, there must be one hundred opinions about every topic. Each and every one of us lives out the self that is only the self with our own particular way of viewing things in our own particular world. In spite of this fact, we believe that the same money and the same society exist objectively outside of ourselves. We accept worldly conventions such as people getting a certain amount of money as a bonus each year. In other words, we live treating many layers of abstract concepts as if they were real. Money, the cup, society; we treat every imaginable thing this way. The number of layers of concepts we fabricate is not one or two, but hundreds or thousands.

Fabrication of abstract concepts is like clouds in the sky. The clouds do not exist as we imagine them to exist, yet we cannot say that clouds do not exist. They do exist. People these days are heavenly beings who live in clouds. Although the life of heavenly beings is comfortable, in Buddhist cosmology it is said that they feel sadness because there are five things that cause them to fall from the clouds. When they grow old their feather garments wear out. Sometimes the clouds also become thinner, and consequently they tumble down to earth.

People who live in clouds can't help but fall when the clouds disappear. As long as they dwell in clouds of concepts, they live in this kind of precarious condition.

Sawaki Roshi often said, "Everyone runs helter-skelter in the great hubbub going on in the world. But this is nothing but scrambling for clouds." This is an interesting way of describing it. In our society, our life consists of scrambling for clouds. The clouds will inevitably disappear sooner or later. Then, when people fall, the higher they are the more painful the shock. Look at the Shah of Iran. He thought he was the great emperor of a rich country that earned a tremendous amount of money because of its oil production. Yet his throne was taken from him, and he went into exile, moving from country to country: America, Panama, Egypt. He must have been really shocked.

The six realms of samsara are simply the way people live, losing touch with the reality of life, floating around in space. These six realms are hell, the realms of hungry ghosts, animals, titans, human beings, and heavenly beings. People lose their heads by treating abstract concepts as if they were real. The six realms are a measurement of the degree to which one does this.

Satori is getting our feet on the ground of the reality of life before we fall from the clouds. The phrases "actualizing enlightenment" and "actualizing anuttara samyak sambodhi" refer to this.

How do we live on the ground of the reality of life in a concrete way, rather than living with our heads in the clouds of concepts? We see a cup, society, and money in our own particular world. In this whole world, north, east, south, and west, no matter where we look we see nothing but our self. Instead of living in the world that is shared by all of us, the self lives in a world in which there is nothing but the self. This oneness of the world and self is dharma. Both "wondrous dharma" and "buddha-dharma" refer to this.

Seen from the point of view of absolute reality, every one of us was born holding our own world. As soon as we are born, we have a world in which there is nothing but our own self. We are born and live holding our own world. When we die, the world in which there is nothing but our self also dies with us.

In Buddhism, life like this, which is only self, is called *shin*. Therefore, mind (*shin*) and dharma (*ho*) are never divided into two. The world that we experience (dharma) and our life experience (mind) are not two, nondual. Mind or subject (*shin*) and dharma or object (*ho*) are one reality. In other words, one mind is all dharma, and all dharma is one mind.

On hearing the word *mind*, we automatically associate it with the psychological mind or consciousness. Sometimes the word is used in this way, but in many cases it means that the mind of one mind is all the myriad dharmas, all the myriad dharmas are one mind. I use the word *life* for the modern sense of the word *mind*. This life is not physiological life but the fundamental life that animates all physiological life, whether it is psychological or physical. This is the one mind.

In other words, by living my own life, all things come to exist in my own world. By living my life, all things are able to exist, and I create a world in which I live. For this reason, one mind (my life) is all the myriad dharmas (all beings). At the same time, I am living out my life experience of this world. Therefore, all the myriad dharmas are this one mind.

At this moment I am looking at all of your different faces and they are reflected in my eyes. However, the basis of this function is simply that since I am living, you are able to exist and are reflected in my retinas. After all, there is nothing but my self. Each and every one of you is also living out your self that is only your self.

This is called jijuyu zanmai. The self receives and uses the self. Jijuyu zanmai is living out the self that is nothing but the self, without losing sight of this jijuyu (the self receiving and using the self).

YOU ARE IN TROUBLE IF YOU THINK, "I WILL REALLY BE SOMEBODY IF I DO ZAZEN AND ATTAIN ENLIGHTENMENT."

If we look at it logically, jijuyu zanmai is the self that is only the self, so basically it cannot be transmitted from one person to another. I am just me. You are just you. Shakyamuni is just Shakyamuni. There is no way that the dharma was transmitted from Shakyamuni to Mahakashyapa. Yet the wonder of zazen is that although Shakyamuni is sitting the self that is only the self, when Mahakashyapa sits zazen in the very same way, Mahakashyapa also becomes the self that is only the self.

This is the reason why Dōgen Zenji said in the first paragraph, "All buddha-tathagatas together have been simply transmitting wondrous dharma and actualizing anuttara samyak sambodhi for which there is an unsurpassable, un-fabricated, wondrous method. This wondrous dharma, which has been transmitted only from buddha to buddha without deviation, has as its criterion jijuyu zanmai." Zazen is the standard.

He also says the same thing with "For all ancestors and buddhas who have been dwelling in and maintaining buddha-dharma, practicing upright sitting in jijuyu zanmai is the true path for opening up enlightenment."

Jijuyu zanmai, in other words the reality of the life of the self that is only the self, is far beyond any comparison. Consequently, even though the expression "actualizing enlightenment" is used, it does not mean that I am enlightened but someone else is deluded. Comparisons like this have nothing to do with jijuyu zanmai.

It is also mistaken to say "I was deluded but attained enlightenment the instant I heard such and such." The self that is only the self, the present that is only the present, surpasses all comparison.

Sawaki Roshi always said, "Satori is not something to be attained." People who practice kensho Zen insist that no matter what anyone says, it's no use unless one attains enlightenment. In *Bendōwa*, Dōgen Zenji also used the expression "actualizing" or "attaining enlightenment." People who practice for the purpose of gaining enlightenment through kensho Zen often cite this phrase.

However, Buddhist terms are completely beyond comparison. In Buddhism, words are used in a decisive and absolute way.

For example, when we say "big" in Buddhism, we mean big in an absolute way. An elephant is bigger than a human being. A whale is bigger than an elephant. But *big* when used in Buddhist terminology is different. A whale just swims in a puddle on the earth. Is the earth big? No! The earth is just a speck of dust floating around the sun. Well, is the solar system big? The solar system is just a spot in the Milky Way galaxy. And there are supposed to be an infinite number of galaxies in the universe. Comparison is beside the point in Buddhism.

The other day I finally found the Andromeda nebula with a pair of binoculars. I look at it with my whole heart every night. In the old days, the world was much bigger, yet recently it has gotten smaller. In the past, animals such as raccoons and foxes played active parts in Japanese fairy tales, and we enjoyed them. We had a lot of romantic dreams then. But now, this is no longer possible in Japan. Japan is jammed with cars. Countries outside Japan, like Tibet, were mysterious realms, and the Arctic and Antarctic were unknown worlds. Mount Everest was thought to be unconquerable, and the sun and moon were objects of worship. But now, because of the development of science and technology, there is no place left that we cannot reach. Things have really changed within the past fifty years. The possibility of knowing everything now exists, so we have lost our dreams. I feel the earth has become smaller and our life has become dull. That is why, when I found the Andromeda nebula with my binoculars, I was delighted. It is just a dim distant shape, but I was so happy to see it. There are supposed to be billions of such nebulas in the universe, so we feel that space is really huge.

Yet if we think it over, it is not so simple. Space is huge only when we think and compare it with other things. We cannot judge what is big and what is small in this way.

"Boundless and unlimited" in Buddhism means absolutely boundless and unlimited beyond any comparison. The often-used term *maha* (big) means surpassing any comparison.

This is also true when we think about being old. We cannot simply say that something old is something good. For example, at Eiheiji monastery they attach importance to old traditional rituals. Yet if we use the concept of being old in a comparative way, it is completely removed from the buddha-dharma. When they eat at Eiheiji, they observe the old customs and use lacquered wooden bowls (*oryoki*). But if they truly feel "the older the better," they should be using big iron bowls as the monks do in South Asian countries. They also use wooden spoons and chopsticks when they eat. Yet this custom began in Chinese monasteries, or perhaps even Dōgen Zenji started it. If "the older the better" is true, they should eat in the Indian manner, using their fingers. It is said that Indian people can taste with their fingers before they actually put the food in their mouth. Yet in Japan, we eat with wooden spoons and chopsticks. At Eiheiji if they really think old tradition itself is important and should not be changed, they should eat with their fingers as the Buddha did. If they want to find even older ways, they can just chomp the way a chimpanzee or a gorilla does. I guess the oldest table manners are the way an amoeba eats.

As long as we think in this comparative way, discussion becomes endless, and we cannot draw any definite conclusion. This is not Buddhism. If we use the word *old* in the Buddhist sense, it must be old beyond any comparison.

For example, there is a chapter called *Kokyō* (Old mirror) in *Shōbōgenzō*. This old mirror does not mean being old in the sense of time or age. It means being eternal beyond comparison.

In the same way, we must be careful when we use words like *kaigo* (to attain enlightenment) or *genjō* (to actualize or manifest). *Gen*, literally meaning "to appear," does not mean that something that was not previously there suddenly appears. It means that eternal reality, which cannot be hidden nor revealed, which neither exists nor ceases to exist, must be actualized right here, right now. Also *kai* (to open) does not mean that something that had been closed is opened. Even when we use the expression "to attain enlightenment," it does not mean that someone who has been deluded becomes enlightened. We actualize the enlightenment that is inherent in each one of us. This is the meaning of attaining enlightenment. The Buddhist usage of the term is very difficult to understand.

According to popular writers like Kato Totsudo (1872–1949) of the Meiji era, Buddhism teaches us to attain enlightenment by transforming delusion. However, this is not correct. It may be easier to understand, but it is not what Buddhism teaches. We have difficulty understanding this point in the buddha-dharma when we look at it in our usual comparative way. Yet if we try to make it easy to grasp, it turns out to be something different from Buddhism. The idea of transforming delusion to attain enlightenment is easy to understand in terms of our ordinary way of thinking, yet it is not in accord with the buddha-dharma. In Buddhism, the dichotomy of delusion and enlightenment is transcended from the very beginning. We have to practice and actualize right now, right here the buddha-dharma (reality of life) that transcends both delusion and enlightenment. This is Great Enlightenment (*daigo*).

Therefore, from the first, we are neither deluded nor enlightened. Reality itself exists before we divide and name delusion and enlightenment. We are practicing this reality right here and right now. This is called attaining or actualizing enlightenment (*kaigo*). We practice with enlightenment as our base. Practice and enlightenment are simply one (*shushō ichinyo*).

Consequently, a confused attitude such as that I am deluded, or enlightened, or I was deluded and now I am enlightened, is not jijuyu zanmai. Since we are the self that is only the self, surpassing the dichotomy of delusion and enlightenment, we sit in the self that is only the self. This is jijuyu zanmai. This is the true meaning of "actualizing enlightenment." Dōgen Zenji says in *Shōbōgenzō Genjōkōan*, "When you attain one dharma, you are proficient in one dharma; when you encounter one practice, you carry out one practice." Since what we are encountering now is the reality of life, we live it right here. This is the attitude of jijuyu zanmai, and we continue practicing with this attitude until the end.

Why is zazen the reality of life or jijuyu zanmai? In our everyday life, we carry on accepting the kinds of concepts I mentioned previously. We stop this when we sit zazen and let go of thought.

In *Shōbōgenzō Zuimonki*, we find that zazen itself is the practice of Buddha. Zazen itself is nondoing (*fui*). This zazen itself is the real form of the self. To sit zazen is to stop believing concepts—nondoing, or no fabrication. This is the real self that you will see when you actually practice zazen.

People often ask, "Are desires eliminated when we sit zazen?" There is no time when our desires or thoughts stop welling up. As long as we are human, various kinds of thoughts come up no matter how hard we practice zazen. Since it is quiet when we sit, thoughts come up much more than usual. If you are a rich person, you may think that you have to check your bank balance. We who have nothing to do with either money or social status think about women. My disciples at Antaiji are still young, so it must be hard for them. When they sit, they probably think more about women than they do about koans. A woman's face appears as if it were real; we talk with her, we imagine grasping her hands, and so on. Yet when we become aware of the reality that we are doing zazen, we come back to zazen. Then the thoughts coming up in our head disappear in an instant. It is interesting because the fantasies disappear immediately, and only the wall remains in front of our eyes. You will see this when you sit. To experience this is zazen.

Therefore, you will understand clearly that from the point of view of the reality of life, the thoughts we have been caught up in are nothing more than secretions from our brains. It is just scenery painted by the secretions from our brains.

Only when we sit zazen can we understand this clearly, yet it is so difficult to see it in our usual day-to-day life. Ordinarily, we believe that those thoughts in our head are the master of the self. We abstract and reify the fantasies secreted from our brains and are convinced that they are substantial. We take it for granted that what we think is reality. As a result, our original life is bound hand and foot by the fantasies.

Actually, what binds our self hand and foot is nothing but reified concepts or secretions from our brains. For this reason, when we let go of our thoughts, they disappear immediately. It would be interesting if somehow we could make it into a movie. A person who is caught up with money, women, status, or power, and bound hand and foot, becomes free as soon as he lets go of thought. The rope that binds him is immediately cut off, and he is released.

This is a matter of fact. When you sit zazen and let go of thoughts, any kind of thought disappears. All kinds of thoughts can be released if we do not grasp them. When we see things from the ground of this letting go of thoughts, we can clearly see that all thoughts are nothing other than secretions from our brains.

People have a preconception about attaining enlightenment that someone who has been deluded becomes enlightened through some kind of sudden experience, and that person will never be deluded again. This is not true. When you sit and let go of thoughts right now, you can certainly do it. At that moment, all restraints that bind you hand and foot disappear at once. This is attaining enlightenment. However, on the next day, the woman's face again appears. It will appear again and again, not on the next day but today, or even the next moment. So it is not true that if you attain enlightenment once, you finish the great matter and you need not practice anymore. As long as there is life, a kind of ready-made enlightenment does not work. Dried, frozen, or preserved enlightenment is no good. The enlightenment you attained yesterday has already passed away today. Consequently, where you practice continuously, right here, right now, moment by moment, you actualize enlightenment. To practice this attaining enlightenment until the end of the world is vital.

However, we ordinary people have a desire to abstract and reify even this enlightenment. We want to gain some enlightenment that is valid until we die. So people want to visit some roshi and receive *inka*, a verification that they have finished practice, so that they can print it on their name cards to show others that they are enlightened ones. Yet when you have such a desire to gain some fixed enlightenment, you are out of jijuyu zanmai.

The reality of life is not something fixed; it is vivid, fresh, and vigorous. We always practice and actualize it right now, right here. We should not reify the concept of enlightenment.

By the way, we cannot say that we can never expect some effect such as becoming bold or courageous as a result of a practice that seeks after enlightenment. It is the same as the case of an athlete who trains himself; he will become more capable as a matter of course.

I make it a rule to take a walk along the banks of the Uji River every day. Lately I see a lot of people jogging. Among them are people who are as fat as a broiler chicken, and others who are as skinny as a deity of poverty. I made a haiku:

Even broilers and deities of poverty
are jogging
these days.

I wonder whether it is good for them to jog, or not? People who are as fat as broilers should do some exercise before they become so fat. And people who are as skinny as a deity of poverty must have something wrong with their lungs or heart, so they had better not push themselves to run. Yet these days, since it is said that jogging is good for health, everyone has begun to do it. This is the reification of concepts.

On the contrary, if young people practice for a marathon and train themselves as hard as possible, then their legs and heart become stronger, and to that extent the discipline has an effect.

In the same way, if we practice zazen for our own power, such as seeking to become bolder, it might be possible for us to feel bolder or courageous. However, this is the same as the athlete. Although hard training makes him more capable, the effect has a limitation. It has nothing to do with the life that lives and dies. It does not help you when you have to face the matter of life and death.

Consider whether or not athletes can continue to play forever. For example, once when I was a kid I was taken to the Kōdōkan, the headquarters of judo. I saw Kanō Jigorō sitting upright in front of the dōjō. Although he looked just like a small, old man, he was a tenth-grade judo player and called "the great master." That was in the Taisho era [1912–1926]. Though only a child, I thought that he must be the greatest and strongest, because he surveyed the huge men who were playing judo matches there in such a dignified manner. However, later I heard that in both judo and kendo (Japanese fencing), players who are at the fifth or sixth grade (in their middle twenties or thirties at most) are the strongest. Those in the seventh, eighth, or ninth grades are respected because of their careers, yet they are not strong anymore. I guess Kanō Jigorō was not so strong when I saw him.

When I was a kid, storybooks on samurai were very popular. I remember a story of Tsukahara Bokuden and Miyamoto Musashi. Bokuden, the old master of kendo, was living by himself in a hermitage in the deep mountains. One day when Bokuden was cooking, Musashi, still a young samurai, sneaked in and suddenly attacked Bokuden from behind with a sword. Bokuden parried the sword with a pot lid, then held the young samurai down. I admired him and was convinced that only a master could pull such a stunt. Yet now I think it must not be true. In the first place, it is impossible to receive a sword strike with a wooden pot lid. If he tried, he would have been slashed. But in storybooks everything is exaggerated and told as if such a feat could be accomplished by result of hard training. As for reality, no matter how strong or skillful a man was when young, when he becomes old he loses vigor. There is a proverb that says, "In the end, a flying arrow shot from a strong crossbow does not pierce through a thin sheet of silk cloth." In reality, capability attained through discipline loses its power when a person becomes old and decrepit.

I feel this deeply when I remember Sawaki Roshi's closing years. Sawaki Roshi had a big voice. He often said that he had never lost the will to lay down his life in the battlefield. He was a brave warrior during the Russo-Japanese War of 1904–1905. Once the fighting was so fierce that even a battalion commander shrank back. At that time, although he was a mere private first class, Sawaki Roshi rushed out yelling "Forward!" Then all the others followed him, a private first class at the head of a battalion. Sawaki Roshi was a man of pluck long before he became a Zen monk. His voice was also tremendously loud. When I was practicing under him he was already quite old, but when he got angry and scolded others in a voice of thunder, people could not help feeling as if the whole temple building was quaking. However, in his closing years, his voice became very thin. When visitors talked with him they could not hear his voice clearly, and I had to translate for him.

After all, human capability is like that. Therefore it is not bad to train physically or mentally, but such capability is not helpful at all when we encounter a matter of life and death. It has nothing to do with life, which includes birth, old age, sickness, and death. We have to realize that the zazen that Dōgen Zenji taught must be clearly distinguished from such training for the sake of having much nerve. There are some people who practice zazen as a discipline for the sake of becoming courageous. I predict that the technique of using zazen as training for the sake of becoming brave, of eliminating delusions, or of concentrating one's mind will be studied by psychologists, and those techniques will be put to use in psychotherapy, which is very popular now in America. This is not bad.

However, Dōgen Zenji's zazen has nothing to do with such techniques for psychotherapy. It is a religion that shows us the true way of life. Yet I think the time will come, within a few decades or centuries, when the word *religion* will also die out, because as soon as we use the word *religion* some peculiar atmosphere arises. *Religion* is a kind of disgusting word. I hope this word will fall into disuse.

Dōgen Zenji's zazen is simply the most fundamental matter of our life. It is the matter of the life of one's self, which is born, lives, and dies. Therefore, it is essentially different from the kinds of zazen used as training for conventional and worldly purposes. I want you to understand this thoroughly. This matter of life that is born, lives, and dies, is not a matter of individuals separated from other individuals. This is the matter of the self that is only the self, the present that is only the present of each and every one of us who lives out our own life.

Self-power training is a matter of individuality in which "I" train myself; I become enlightened and a great person. Shinran Shōnin, the founder of the Jōdo Shin School, called such people *jajoshu* (those who are wrongly established), and called people who have faith in other-power *shōjōshū* (those who are rightly established). Basically, he said that self-power training is not right. In the same sense, the word *kaigo* (attaining enlightenment) does not mean that some "I" trains myself and I become enlightened for a human purpose. True *kaigo* means that we actualize the life that transcends delusion and enlightenment.

In the Jōdo Shin School, they use the expression "determined faith." I think there is a time when one settles down in faith and never doubts anymore. What does this mean? According to our common sense, we firmly believe that our own thought is absolutely correct and the only measure of all things. But instead we settle ourselves in this faith, and never doubt that our thoughts are nothing more than secretions from our brain, which cannot be a yardstick. Instead of thinking that our thoughts are true, we can actually let go of our thoughts. In that world we see everything as the reality of life, which is reforming the self. This is determined faith. When we see reality after reforming the self, the world that is seen through our thoughts is an illusory world. Prince Shōtoku (574–621, a very important early Japanese Buddhist patron, scholar, and practitioner) said that the world is illusory, and only the Buddha is real. This means that reality is seen from the ground of letting go of thought; that is, just life itself is of highest value. When you understand this, your eyes of faith open.

When your eyes open to reality, you cannot help arousing an awareness that is disgusted by this dirty, illusory world and seeks after the Pure Land. Since this world is illusory, it is by nature defiled and incorrect. People of Pure Land Buddhism view the world from the perspective that only the world of Amitabha Buddha is real. They measure things by seeing with the eyes of Amitabha Buddha. This is very important.

Each and every one of us has many different kinds of problems in our day-to-day life. There is no one without anguish or anxiety. But it is necessary to reflect upon our anguish and anxiety with buddha's eye. When we see things with buddha's eyes, we will find that we are perplexed by trifles. We suffer from what we do not need to suffer from, and we do not suffer from what we must suffer from. When we reconsider our perplexity or suffering from this direction, we will be able to find comfort. With buddha's eye, we see that ordinary people do not worry about that which human beings should worry about. We must repeatedly reflect upon and reconsider this essential point of our practice.

By the way, there is a group of people who have complicated brains. They would say that it is not bad to have such an attitude toward faith, yet isn't it also a secretion from our brain to think of seeing from the buddha's eye? This doubt may arise in their minds.

Now I am going to talk about a really difficult matter. If you want to listen to a simple talk, you had better go to Seichō no Ie or Sōka Gakkai [modern popular Japanese Buddhist groups]. Their ideas are very easy to understand. I think you are here because you are not satisfied with such shallow teachings. I also talk for the sake of people who have complicated brains and are, so to speak, deeply deluded, and who do not believe what they are taught without questioning. Consequently, my talk will become difficult to understand. Please be patient.

Having faith means believing that things seen through one's own eyes are not real, but things seen by buddha's eye are real. However, if you think that believing this is also nothing but a kind of thought, you overturn the idea. This is doubting. But the idea is overturned yet again when you let go of the doubt, because such a doubt itself is nothing other than a thought. It is an interesting world. You can let go of such doubts, too. This is determined faith. No matter what kind of thought it is, it will fall away when we let go. This is where the whole world of zazen opens.

It is said in *Shōbōgenzō Zanmai Ō Zanmai* (The samadhi of the king of samadhis), "We must know that the whole world of zazen and the whole world of other things are totally different. Realizing this, we must clarify and affirm the arousing of bodhi-mind; practice; awakening; and the nirvana of buddhas and ancestors."

Understanding deeply and clarifying how different the whole world of zazen and the whole world of other things are from each other, as a buddha one has to clarify and affirm "the arousing of bodhi-mind; practice; awakening; and the nirvana of buddhas and ancestors" in the world of zazen. When we arouse bodhi mind (aspiration for the Way), we must do it from the ground of letting go of thought. We must do the practice and actualize the awakening and the nirvana of letting go of thought.

From the beginning, it is completely different from the arousing of aspiration, practice, and attaining enlightenment of ordinary human beings who try to make the egocentric "I" greater. If you practice zazen because you want to become plucky and courageous like Saigō Takamori or Katsu Kaishu (Japanese heroes), your attitude is totally different from the aspiration, practice, awakening, and nirvana of the buddhas and ancestors. After all, as a foundation for determined faith, there must be jijuyu zanmai, which actualizes the reality of life through just doing zazen. In that sense, the teaching of other-power (*tariki*) of Shinran Shōnin is a good attitude for faith. It is grounded in buddha-dharma.

However, there are a lot of people who are deeply deluded and cannot enter the faith of other-power. For those people, just sitting zazen is the easiest practice, because as soon as they sit zazen right now, right here, the world of zazen will open. Yet even if you sit zazen, it can be overturned into self-power (*jiriki*) practice, depending exclusively upon your attitude toward zazen. Realizing this thoroughly, you must practice zazen on the basis of letting go of thought.

For us zazen practitioners, determination and faith is important. We have to believe that even though we do not understand it, zazen is the reality of life. And when we actually sit zazen, we should not think that we are sitting good zazen. If you think so, it is a mere thought. So sitting from the ground of letting go of thought is even letting go of thoughts that we are doing good zazen. Consequently, we cannot know whether we are doing good zazen or not. When we sit zazen, in this sense, our faith must be settled.

It is not necessary to discuss such complicated things as mentioned above. It is good enough if you just sit zazen. Yet I think you are all deeply deluded and have a lot of doubts before becoming convinced, so I am talking about how we should deal with those doubts.

I would like to talk a little more on a deeply deluded matter. I think human beings have two sorts of eyes. One is the eye of thought; another is the eye that goes beyond human thoughts. The view through the eye of thought puts thought as the foundation of all things and firmly believes that its own thought is the measure for all things. This is the eye of ordinary human beings.

We often hear of troubles caused by marriage, especially in the countryside. For example, a son from a rich family falls in love with a woman and asks his parents' permission to marry her. His parents say, "No! A woman from a poor family like hers is not a good match because of the status of our family."

This assessment coming up in the parents' minds

becomes an absolute for them. From my point of view, family standing is not so noble that they should be proud of it. It is not a big deal. If they broaden their view, their family status is not so different from that of the woman's family. Although there is no reason to be against their son's marriage, they attach themselves to their idea of their family standing. As a final outcome, the trouble may become bigger and bigger until their son leaves his family or even commits suicide. They have a preconception and take it for granted that something that is of no value objectively is tremendously valuable subjectively. This is the way ordinary human beings view things.

Such a subjective way of viewing things through our own narrow eyes is not right. The right way of seeing things must be objective and rational. This is the way modern science sees things. It was brought forward by the Greek philosophers. What is the basis of objective observation? According to Kant, it is Ego as a general concept. The scientific way of viewing things is based upon this thinking. What is the Ego as a general concept? It is not a mere individual "I" but a universal "I." For example, I call myself "I"; you call yourself "I"; we set up the general concept of "I" or ego. The scientific way of seeing things is based upon general concepts, the root of modern science. From the viewpoint of science, when science improves, all problems we have now will be resolved. This is an idea held by many people in this science-oriented society. However, it is not in reality true.

Concepts of thought are abstractions. If abstract thought pursues the reality of life, it will be endless. Even if it is pursued to the atom, it cannot reach an end. You can cut one thing in half, and cut it in half again, and again, continuing to cut it in half infinitely. Even when it becomes as small as an atom, you still can cut it in half. It never becomes zero. You could add an infinite number of zeros after the decimal, yet it never becomes zero. As long as there is one at the end of an infinite number of zeros, if we enlarge that, it could still make a huge difference. Maybe scientists today assume that when they analyze things down to an atom, they can reach the reality of life. Yet no matter how science develops, scientists will be caught seeking it in the gap between zero and the one far after the decimal point. That is all they can do.

It is impossible for a general concept of "I" to resolve all problems. Both the eyes of a subjective "I" and the eyes of an objective and reasonable "I" are the same, because both of them are the eyes of thought.

There is another eye from ancient times, the eye that does not assume that egocentric thought is absolute. This is the eye of religion, which believes that instead of our thought, only God is the true eye. However, since this eye negates all thought and human reason, it is possible for it to become one with superstitious false belief. People might think, "In the Bible it is said that leprosy and paralysis were healed by prayer. The Bible is absolutely right. Therefore, when we have some serious disease, we should not go to a hospital. We should heal it by prayer." Even the way of reading the Bible can become fanatical depending upon our attitudes. I think this is not the right way either.

In the case of Buddhism, though, it is different. The buddha's eye is that of letting go of thought. It does not negate thoughts. We just let them come and go freely. This is practice that is actual activity. When we put letting go of thought into words, someone who is a philosopher might say that it is also a kind of thought. However, we have to let go of even such doubting thought. The practice of zazen as letting go of thought is an actual activity grounded in life instead of thoughts or concepts.

As I said before, we have two kind of eyes. One is the eye of thought; the other is the eye that negates thoughts. When we consider these two eyes with thoughts or concepts, they absolutely contradict each other. Yet if we see them in the practice of letting go of thought in the ground of life, they never contradict each other.

In the ground of reality of life as practice, our brain

belongs to life. Life animates our brain and enables it to function. Consequently, in our practice of zazen we should not negate or eliminate our thoughts, because thoughts are just secretions from our brain.

Christianity and other religions negate our thoughts or reasoning because they believe our thoughts are evil and only God is true. Then there is a danger of accepting superstition or false belief. On the contrary, in our practice of zazen, we just let go of thought in the ground of life that animates our brain and enables it to function.

When we drive a car safely, we do not handle the steering wheel and the brake pedal after thinking in our brain that we have to deal with these various things. Naturally and freely we keep away from other cars in the opposite lane, or push the brake pedal when we see a pedestrian. This is the way our brain functions in life.

We should drive our life safely in the same way we drive a car. The eye of thought is like driving a car with tension. For example, since I have no experience, if I drive a car I will be tense and even frightened, fearful of what is happening. It is dangerous, so I do not drive a car. On the other hand, if you negate your thought and leave everything to God, it is like driving a car with your eyes closed. This is also dangerous.

Driving a car by letting go of thought means putting your brain as life into full function. When we sit zazen, our brain must be wide awake instead of being spaced out. Yet we should let go of thought and drive freely. We have to drive our life in this way.

I don't mean that you should not practice zazen unless you understand and memorize what I am saying, and keep it in your mind when you actually sit. Rather you must just sit, letting go of even those thoughts I've discussed. That is all.

The Basis of All Value Lies in the Fact: "I am Living." Then, What Is the Reality of Life of the Self?

What we actually do in sitting zazen as jijuyu zanmai is let go of thought, which reifies abstract concepts, and live out the actual life that is the oneness of the self and of the world of our own life experience.

We must be careful to understand that the self that is only the self is not mere self-consciousness. Do not misunderstand. This is the self even when we let go of self-consciousness. It is interesting, isn't it? In common sense, we believe that we exist only because we are conscious of our selves. However, in reality, the self exists even when we let go of self-consciousness. It would be interesting if the self ceased to exist when we sat zazen and let go of thought, in the same way as snow melts on a heating stove. Instead, only when we let go of thought does the real self appear. This is important. Doing zazen is nothing but actually experiencing this. So in doing zazen, the self that lives life experience (mind) and the world that is lived as life experience (dharma) are not two, but one. This is the absolute one reality before any division into two.

This is the meaning of "one mind is all the myriad dharmas; all the myriad dharmas are one mind." This is the reality of life of the self.

In just practicing this absolute reality of life, I am just I. Shakyamuni is just Shakyamuni. Mahakashyapa is just Mahakashyapa. When they sit zazen they are just themselves, and yet they become one in the fact that both of them are just living out the self that is only the self. This is the way the wondrous dharma of the reality of life is correctly transmitted. In the same way, it has been transmitted from one to another up to the present day. This is the buddha-dharma. This is why Dōgen Zenji said "practicing proper sitting in jijuyu zanmai has been the true way to actualize enlightenment."

According to the unmistakenly handed down tradition.

The Japanese word for tradition is *shūmon*. The Chinese character *shu* means the essence or the most important thing. *Mon* means a gate. In general usage, *shūmon* is a school or a sect that is a gate for entering the truth. Yet here this *shūmon* or tradition does not mean the Zen sect as one of the schools of Buddhism; it means the center of the buddha-dharma. In other words, it is zazen that has been transmitted among the followers of Bodhidharma as the buddha-dharma itself.

According to that tradition, it is said,

The straightforward buddha-dharma that has been simply transmitted is supreme among the supreme.

The buddha-dharma is transmitted from the self that is only the self to the self that is only the self. Such directly transmitted dharma is supreme beyond comparison. We always attach ourselves to something that we think relatively better or more valuable than other things, and we are blinded to real life by that. We must purify our system of value. For living out our own life, we must first of all clarify absolute value. Many people live for fulfillment of their desires. These people are like chickens at a poultry farm. I feel sorry for the chickens that just eat nutritious feed day and night and lay as many eggs as possible. This is all that they do in their lives. Chicken raisers keep the light on in the chicken coop all night to keep the chickens producing eggs efficiently. They calculate how many eggs can be laid by one chicken, and they kill the chickens when they become old.

People who pursue money, power, efficiency, delicious food, drinking, and playing as the most valuable things are no different from chickens. We must clearly understand what is of supreme value in our lives. This is a crucial matter.

I wrote on my New Year's greeting card this year that the life of the self in life and death is the be-all and end-all. The fact is that "I," which is alive and going to die, exists as the basis here and now only when I exist and my world in which I live exists. Such a world of the self that is only the self is the only basis for a system of value.

I say to my disciples that by all means, they should sit zazen silently for ten years. If they go through ten years, I will say sit another ten years. When they sit for twenty years, I will say sit ten more years. Anyway, we must sit silently for at least ten years.

One minute of zazen is one minute of Buddha. Your first zazen is your first sitting Buddha. That is good zazen. You don't need to accumulate experiences to do true zazen. However, the reason I tell them to sit silently for ten years is that because we are usually apt to think that gaining money, power, or fame is good; we have to go through long practice before we can truly convince ourselves that such things are not valuable at all. If you practice zazen for ten or twenty years without concern for money, power, or fame, you will see that there is something more valuable than those things. Otherwise you cannot lead others to practice zazen.

If you practice by yourself, you don't need to practice in such a strict way. Yet what I expect of my disciples is not that, but for them to become locomotives that draw people in throughout the world. To be a locomotive, one should not change one's system of value or direction of life in midstream. For this reason, monks have to sit twenty or thirty years and embody the supreme buddha-dharma to the point where they can see that dharma absolutely unquestionably. This is why I encourage my disciples to sit even if it means going through many difficulties.

From the time you begin practicing with a teacher, the practices of incense burning, bowing, nembutsu, repentance, and reading sutras are not at all essential.

Dōgen Zenji said that when one meets a teacher who is like the previously mentioned locomotive, and begins to receive instruction about zazen, one need not carry on incense burning, bowing, nembutsu, repentance, or reading sutras.

Strictly speaking, Dōgen Zenji said that since chanting nembutsu and reading sutras are nonessential and unnecessary practices, we should not practice them.

There are many people who talk as if they live for the sake of eating brown rice because they have heard that brown rice is good for health. Or someone may say that he will live by eating only vegetables, like a silkworm, because vegetarianism is good for health. For the same reason, people burn incense in front of a buddha statue, bow, chant nembutsu, repent, and recite sutras. When we do these things we become calm, and some people say that it is better to practice things like these. But this way of practice clouds the pure value system. When we are involved in those things, we are apt to take them as the purpose of practice, and we should not practice in that way. From the outset we should not engage in such extra activities, because purifying our system of value is important.

Shinran threw away everything except nembutsu. In the Jōdo Shin School, nembutsu is supreme beyond comparison, so they practice only nembutsu. The important matter is to make our system of value pure.

Just sit, dropping off body and mind.

"Simply" means single-mindedly. Practice zazen single-mindedly and drop off body and mind. In *Hōkyōki* (Dōgen's journals from his study in China), it is said that to practice zazen is to drop off body and mind. Some people say that we should gain satori in order to experience dropping off of body and mind. However, dropping off body and mind should not be misunderstood as a kind of satori experience in which our body and mind seem to disappear. In the later part of *Hōkyōki*, it is said that dropping off body and mind is zazen. This is clearly mentioned. Just to sit wholeheartedly is dropping off body and mind. When we sit, letting go of all thoughts that reify abstract concepts, all things fall off. This is dropping off body and mind.

When one displays the buddha mudra with one's whole body and mind, sitting upright in this samadhi even for a short time, everything in the entire dharma world becomes buddha mudra, and all space in the universe completely becomes enlightenment.

This paragraph is Dōgen Zenji's description of the merit of zazen as jijuyu zanmai. The merit of buddha-dharma is completely different from the merit in a worldly system of value, which is good for nothing in Sawaki Roshi's expression. This is not easy to understand.

Nishiari Zenji (Nishiari Bokusan, 1821–1910; a great modern Sōtō Zen master) often said to his disciples, "Talking about buddha-dharma to you is the same as trying to have a love affair with a kid." I suppose that many of his disciples were forced to become monks by their parents and disliked practice of the buddha way. Once a person becomes a novice, he has to go to a monastery, and while staying there he is forced to practice zazen and listen to lectures on the buddha-dharma. To give a talk on buddha-dharma is really like attempting to have a love affair with a kid. It's really difficult to entice a baby who is not yet sexually awakened to have a love affair.

I am lucky on this point. My disciples at Antaiji were all awakened to bodhi mind and practiced spontaneously. There was no one who stayed in order to get a license to be a priest. Also, all of you who come to listen to my talk here are at least interested in the buddha-dharma and want to practice zazen of your own accord. My talk can be understood by people like you.

Expressions like "letting go of thought" or "dropping off body and mind" become mere concepts or words in literature if the audience has not yet awakened to the way-seeking mind. I read a treatise by a scholar who tried to research the meaning of "dropping off body and mind" by referring to much literature. If you want to refer to literature about "dropping off body and mind," Dōgen Zenji's "dropping off body and mind is zazen" is good enough. Then you can understand that it is nonsense to discuss "dropping off body and mind" without practicing zazen. "Dropping off body and mind," "shikantaza," and "letting go of thought" cannot be understood without actually letting go of thought in the practice of zazen right now, right here.

"When one displays buddha mudra with one's whole body and mind" means with one's three kinds of actions:

physical, verbal, and mental. We sit in full lotus with our body, put our tongue against the roof of our mouth and keep silent, and mentally we do not seek to become a buddha but put aside the operation of our intellect, volition, and consciousness. This is to display buddha mudra with one's whole body and mind.

That "sitting upright in this samadhi even for a short time, everything in the entire dharma world becomes buddha mudra," is really wonderful. When we sit in proper form in samadhi, the whole universe of sitting, the world of zazen, opens. The world of zazen is completely different from the world of other things.

Usually we only think of saving secret money for our own sake in the moneybag of our thoughts. We are happy when we put some savings in our moneybag, secretly thinking it is our possession. Let go of this secret savings of thought. Then the world of life opens. The self that is only the self is the self letting go of thought. When we let go of saving our thoughts, we are in the world of reality of life. This is what is meant by "everything in the entire dharma world becomes buddha mudra." This is the world of "one mind is all the myriad dharmas; all the myriad dharmas are one mind."

"All space in the universe completely becomes enlightenment." The word *enlightenment* differs from the commonly used word, *satori*. If you say that you got enlightened, your enlightenment is nothing but a kind of personal savings.

Enlightenment is not personal savings; enlightenment is letting go of thought that claims things as mine. Casting aside the discrimination between enlightenment and delusion, the reality of life is enlightenment in its true sense. We must understand that when Dōgen Zenji uses words like *satori* or *kaigo* (to attain satori), the words do not mean "enlightenment" like personal savings.

Therefore, it enables buddha-tathagatas to increase the dharma joy of their own original grounds, and renew the adornment of the way of awakening.

This means that all buddhas naturally exist in the pleasure of being buddhas. They let go of personal savings and stand on the ground of life. When we examine the final settlement of our accounts of the reality of life, living out the reality of life through letting go of thought makes the reality of life richer.

This may not be a good example, but if a wife takes secret savings from her husband's salary and gets interest of four or five percent, while on the other hand her husband borrows money at high interest, eventually they lose their money and may have to flee in the night.

When I lived in Ogaki, I saw the Red Flag at a big spinning company, Daikōbō. The employees of the company went on strike for higher wages. While the dispute was dragging on, their slogan changed from demanding higher wages to not selling the factory. Unfortunately, it was during a depression in the textile industry, and, since it was a long dispute, the company didn't honor its bills. In the end, the company went under, and the big factory was sold, with the land becoming an empty lot. When we calculate on the basis of personal savings, things go in that way.

Our attitude should be different: no personal savings. When each one of us lets go of all kinds of thoughts, both family and company become rich. In the same manner, on the basis of letting go of thought, the reality of life becomes rich as the reality of life. This is the meaning of "increasing the dharma joy of their own original grounds."

Simultaneously, all living beings of the dharma world in the ten directions and six realms become clear and pure in body and mind, realize great emancipation, and their own original face appears.

The dharma world of the ten directions means all worlds in the east, west, south, north, northeast, northwest, southeast, southwest, up, and down. The six realms are the realms of hell, hungry ghosts, animals, titans, human beings, and heavenly beings. These six realms are the measurement of how we human beings are involved in delusion and pulled by desires. As ordinary human beings, each one of us believes that our thoughts are the lord of ourselves, and thinking in this way with our thoughts as our base, we are bound firmly hand and foot by them. The one who is caught up most severely is the dweller in hell, with the degree and nature of binding varying among beings in the other five realms.

"To become clear and pure in body and mind" means to become free from such ignorance and defilement. "To become aware of great emancipation" means to be released from such binding thoughts.

These days, I've heard that some kids commit suicide out of spite when their desires are not fulfilled. From a mature point of view, it is ridiculous to kill yourself over such trifles. However, for a kid it might be natural to think that if he wants this or that and his parents refuse to buy them, he should commit suicide out of spite.

This is an analogy for the difference between a kid and a mature person, but as a matter of fact, from the point of view of a person mature in the buddha-dharma, though we think we are adults, all of us are childish. When we see things with truly mature eyes, there is no need to struggle over money or power. This is what is meant by the saying "to become aware of great emancipation."

"Actualizing their own original face" is actualizing the true reality of life. This wonderful reality of life is inherent in each and every one of us without seeking after it, yet in spite of that fact, since we are bound up by our thoughts, we put up a fuss. This is the scenery of the six realms, but when we sit in zazen, we let go of such thought. This is dropping off body and mind.

I have already repeated that the reality of life is "the one mind is all the myriad dharmas; all the myriad dharmas are one mind." That is, in the reality of life, life experience (mind) and the world that is experienced (dharma) are not two, but one reality. But when we view things from the perspective of dharma (object), "all things (dharmas) together awaken to supreme enlightenment." All the myriad dharmas are themselves nothing but absolute enlightenment.

Absolute enlightenment (anuttara samyak sambodhi) is Shakyamuni's enlightenment. When Shakyamuni attained enlightenment he said, "I and all living beings on the great earth completed the Way together. Mountains, rivers, grass, and trees, all attained buddhahood without exception." He did not say that he became enlightened but the rest of the beings still remained in delusion. When one person attains enlightenment, one mind is all the myriad dharmas, all the myriad dharmas are one mind, and the whole universe of the person's life experience becomes enlightened. This is the reason I say that when we sit in zazen and let go of thought, the whole world suddenly and completely changes.

When Shakyamuni attained enlightenment, all the myriad dharmas within buddha's mind, that is, mountains, rivers, grass, and trees, all became buddha. All are aspects of buddha.

In this sense, each and every one of us has been enlightened by Shakyamuni Buddha. In the Jōdo Shin School, this is expressed as our having already been saved by Amitabha Buddha.

Nevertheless, we ordinary human beings are screaming that we are deluded. Among my disciples, there was a person who had a manic-depressive psychosis. One morning, since he did not come out of his room, I went to him. He was crying "It's dark! It's dark!" Actually, he had covered his eyes with his hands. In the same manner we believe that our thought is our lord and, caught up by our thought, we start to cry, "We are deluded human beings!" Only if we let go of thoughts without any exception can we have bodies that are enlightened by Shakyamuni Buddha and live within the world that is enlightened by Shakyamuni Buddha. This is an absolute fact. In other words, "all things together awaken to supreme enlightenment and utilize buddha-body." This is undoubtedly true.

They immediately go beyond the culmination of awakening

*and sit upright under the kingly bodhi tree. At the same time,
they turn the incomparable great dharma wheel and begin
expressing ultimate and unfabricated profound prajna.*

Without a doubt, all things are nothing other than
buddha's body, yet they are even beyond the buddha's body.
This is what Dōgen Zenji meant when he said that "they go
beyond the culmination of awakening."

In the world of reality, a violet is a violet, a rose is a
rose, good is good, evil is evil, everything is just as it is. This
is what is meant by the expression *shōbō jissō* (all the myriad
dharmas are the true form). All of us, as the reality of life,
are buddha's body, which is ultimate awareness; but none
cling to the ultimate awareness. A violet is just a violet, a
rose is just a rose, good is good, evil is evil.

Doing zazen is not sleeping. Our brain has to be
awake. We cannot say that no thoughts come up, yet if we
let go of the thoughts, we can let go of them. Sometimes we
mindlessly start to think, for example, that we should invest
money in this or that because we would get more profit.
However, when we become aware of the thought and go
back to zazen, there is only a wall in front of us.

During the time of Shakyamuni, zazen was called tree
watching. In ancient India they sat facing a huge tree. I suppose after sitting practice was introduced into China they
started to sit facing a wall. When we let go of thought, only
the wall remains. This is "form is empty." Form (*rupa*)
means "materials" in Buddhist terminology. When we are
sitting in zazen, everything coming up is the scenery within
zazen. Various sorts of thinking well up, but when we let go
of them, there is only a wall in front of us. Form is empty.
Within emptiness there are various things. This is "emptiness is form."

If we practice this zazen continuously, we realize that
what we think in our brain is nothing but secretions from our
brain. Experiencing this is important, for to understand this
is to "express ultimate and unfabricated profound prajna."

"To sit under the kingly bodhi tree" means to sit in the

world of zazen seeing only a tree or a wall. "To be incomparable" means it is beyond comparison or judgments as to what it is equal to and what it is not. That is, it is absolute equality. A violet is a violet, a rose is a rose, without comparison. Everything is as it is. "Ultimate and unfabricated" means that it reaches the most refined way of life and being without man-made defilements. It is zazen in which we live out the reality of life, letting go of thoughts.

There is a path through which the anuttara samyak sambodhi of all things returns [to the person in zazen], and whereby [that person and the enlightenment of all things] intimately and imperceptibly assist each other. Therefore this zazen person without fail drops off body and mind, cuts away previous tainted views and thoughts, awakens genuine buddha-dharma, universally helps the buddha work in each place, as numerous as atoms, where buddha-tathagatas teach and practice, and widely influences practitioners who are going beyond buddha, thereby vigorously exalting the dharma that goes beyond buddha.

To practice zazen as jijuyu zanmai is to sit within the reality of life as "one mind is all the myriad dharmas; all the myriad dharmas are one mind." When we practice this, all the myriad dharmas influence the one mind. This occurs without concern for whether you believe it or not. One mind (my life experience) and all the myriad dharmas (the world that I experience) are not two, but one reality. Therefore, the two help each other. This is the meaning of the "path through which the incomparable awareness of all things returns [to the person in zazen], and [that person and the enlightenment of all things] intimately and imperceptibly assist each other." This can be said to be the case of all the myriad dharmas too, but here it is referring to the one mind.

"Dropping off body and mind" means letting go of thought. When the reality of all the myriad dharmas becomes clear in its aspect as object, our body and mind will naturally drop off, and worthless personal views or thoughts will be completely cut off.

You may think personal views or thoughts are a big

deal, but they are actually insignificant. Putting value on such trifling things, you go astray. In this human world, we cannot always be friendly to everyone. Sometimes we have to go on strike. There is no reason to allow only capitalists to gain profit, so if employers are mean, we should walk out in order to teach them a lesson.

But on the other hand, we should see that such a conflict is a kind of sport. This is the view of a mature person. Neither workers nor employers should take it too seriously. If they fight in complete earnest, as in the case of the spinning company, they will only come to ruin together. Even when we have to go on strike, we should have a mature eye that "cuts away previous tainted views and thoughts." I think this is most important.

"Awakens genuine buddha-dharma" means to be the original true reality of life. "Universally helps the buddha work in each place, as numerous as atoms, where buddha-tathagatas teach and practice," means that even a small entity like an atom becomes a practice place of buddhas and tathagatas.

You may know that there are innumerable small buddha images carved on the platform and the halo of the great image of buddha at Todaiji temple in Nara. Do you know what this means?

Buddha statues are artistic expressions of our zazen. The small buddhas on the platform and the halo of the great buddha mean that each and every action of the zazen person becomes zazen and preaches the dharma. When we practice zazen, all activities are expressions of dharma.

To go beyond buddha means to become buddha and yet never stay in buddhahood. If someone becomes buddha and claims he is a buddha, he is clinging to some view of buddha.

Although they are buddha, they continuously and endlessly go beyond buddha. They must always be vividly alive moment to moment, and not stay within a certain state of satori, saying they have attained enlightenment. They do not become like lifeless, dried fish of satori.

IF THERE IS THE SLIGHTEST GAP BETWEEN ONE'S REALITY AND APPEARANCE, ONE CANNOT BE A HUMAN LIVING IN RELIGION

At this time, because earth, grasses and trees, fences and walls, tiles and pebbles, all things in the dharma realm in ten directions, carry out buddha work, therefore everyone receives the benefit of wind and water movement caused by this functioning, and all are imperceptibly helped by the wondrous and incomprehensible influence of buddha to actualize the enlightenment at hand.

In the previous section, the merit of zazen within the dharma (object) and mind (subject) of a zazen person was described. In this section, Dōgen Zenji talks about the merit of zazen in the conventional world created by our thought, the world in which you and I meet each other.

Once we sit in zazen, our environment actually and completely changes. For example, today you are here. There might be someone who was going to go to a bar to drink with his friends but changed his mind and decided to come to this temple, Sōsenji. In such a case, if he went to go drinking, he might have a few glasses of sake and become cheerful. If a hostess serves him, he would drink more. After a while he would drink more and more, and would not be satisfied with just being served by the hostess and holding her hand. Then he would go deeper and deeper into the world of drink.

In the beginning, a person drinks sake. In the next stage, sake drinks sake, and finally, sake drinks the person.

Yet if you come to Sōsenji to practice zazen instead of going to drink, and you actually sit, the whole world of zazen appears.

Zazen is wondrous. When we think of zazen in the context of the world in which we don't sit (the world of other things), it seems pretty irksome. When we sit, we only have to bring out a cushion and just sit on it, yet we think it a great trouble to do so. But once you begin to sit, your mind changes, and it feels good to do zazen.

You should just sit without thinking anything. To support this, living in a monastery is convenient. When the time comes, the bell for zazen is rung and we sit zazen, setting everything aside without concern for whether we like it or not. We have no time to think it irksome. When we sit, we are obstructed by immovable zazen. In exactly the same way that sake drinks a person, the immovable zazen posture makes a person immovable. When other people are also sitting, it is impossible for only me to stand up and walk around. Dōgen Zenji's expression, "to be obstructed by immovable sitting" is really wonderful. Once we begin to sit, the whole world changes.

In his final days, Sawaki Roshi once accompanied me to Ryūunji temple in Fukui Prefecture. He said, "I am going to visit the temple where I was worshipped while I was sitting. Come with me." When Sawaki Roshi was still a novice, he stayed at this temple. After a *segaki* ceremony during *obon* had been finished (the ceremony to lay to rest uneasy spirits during the summer month when they return), the head priest there told the monks to take the day off. The other monks went to the town of Fukui to have a good time, but Sawaki Roshi did not know what to do in the town; he made up his mind to do zazen. He entered a room in the living quarters of the temple and began to sit zazen. An old woman working for the temple came into the room. She was a nagging old woman who worked her men hard; there are such old women everywhere. She always made novices work like horses. When she opened the sliding door, she was struck dumb with surprise at seeing Sawaki Roshi sitting, and suddenly prostrated herself in front of him as he sat.

Although Roshi was still a boy, he thought that zazen was really wondrous. This experience was one reason Roshi later devoted himself to the practice of zazen and spent his whole life as a practitioner of zazen. There are innumerable people who began to practice zazen because of Sawaki Roshi's influence. I also started to practice zazen because I became his follower, and as a result, here and now I encourage you to practice zazen. The origin of this was that time as a boy, when he once decided to sit. The fact that the old woman prostrated herself in front of his zazen made him practice zazen for his whole life, and I was also tempted into zazen for my whole life. Now you try to do zazen based on listening to my talk. This is really continuous and endless.

Since those who receive and use this water and fire extend the buddha influence of original enlightenment, all who live and talk with these people also share and universally unfold the boundless buddha virtue.

This is completely true. I sit zazen in this moment but it does not die out. There must be people who practice because they were attracted by my practice, and those people will work in the future world. If zazen permeates into the world in this manner, there must come a day when all human beings on the earth will practice zazen. This is practice of the vow, "However innumerable sentient beings are, I vow to save them all."

Without concern as to whether you believe it or not, one mind is all the myriad dharmas; all the myriad dharmas are one mind. A person's action finds an echo in the whole world; an overall trend determines one person's activity. This is the structure of life.

The fact that I sit zazen by myself is a fabulously great matter.

When I was first at Antaiji, I stayed there with Yokoyama Sodō-san. Actually I stayed by myself, and he stayed by himself in separate rooms; Sodō-san sat alone, and I sat alone. That was the reality.

At that time students visited me and often asked, "Why don't you work in society? Why do you sit alone in such an isolated place?" I always replied in this way, "Society always moves without direction. Within such a society it is the greatest contribution to sit immovably by oneself."

When society moves without any direction, if I move in the same way, it becomes all the more entangled and confused. Without being pulled by such movement, I just sit. This is the greatest contribution to society. I have been practicing based on this belief.

My belief came from the way of Bodhidharma's life. The Great Master Bodhidharma came to China from India and exclusively sat facing a wall for nine years. That was his greatest function. Actually, now zazen works widely in the East due to his silent and immovable sitting, and this is not the end. I believe that zazen will someday permeate into all parts of the earth. The origin of this process of evolution is the fact that Bodhidharma came to China and sat silently by himself.

I told my disciples in America to sit silently for ten years. They cannot support themselves through takuhatsu in America. If they did, people would think they were only beggars. So now they are practicing zazen while supporting themselves with part-time jobs. I suppose it is very hard to continue practice for ten years in such a situation. However, if they continue sitting for ten years, I'm sure the situation must change.

They circulate the inexhaustible, ceaseless, incomprehensible, and immeasurable buddha-dharma within and without the whole dharma world.

This is not a false statement. I am living based on this belief.

However, these various things do not mix into the perceptions of this person sitting, because they take place within stillness without any fabrication, and they are enlightenment itself. If practice and enlightenment were separate as people commonly believe, it would be possible for them to perceive each other.

The merit of zazen I mentioned above cannot be grasped by our intellects. We cannot preview what a great contribution zazen will make in the world.

In our common sense we separate practice and enlightenment into two and think that as the result of a certain
amount of zazen practice we can enter such-and-such a state
of mind. Then we smile with satisfaction. If satori is something like personal savings, it is pretty understandable to our
calculating mind.

However, for the followers of Bodhidharma and Dōgen
Zenji, zazen practice is not such a thing. Our zazen is "nonfabrication within stillness" and "zazen itself is enlightenment." We do zazen without expectation of some reward;
we just sit, letting go of everything. Dōgen's *Fukanzazengi*
says, "Let go of all associations and put all affairs aside. Do
not think of either good or evil. Do not be concerned with
either right or wrong." Since our just sitting zazen is limitless and boundless, the merit of zazen cannot be measured
by perception.

I myself, from my long experience of living in a monastery, think the merit of zazen is really wondrous. Even in a
community of practitioners, troubles arise somehow without
any particular reason when we don't sit, for example for a
month during summer vacation. Since the monastery is a
community of people with the same bodhi mind, there
should not be any conflict. Yet as soon as the bodhi mind
becomes even a little bit weak, the world of individual
strangers appears. When we uphold bodhi mind and devote
ourselves to practice and cooperate together, practitioners
become even more intimate with each other than parents or
brothers and sisters. When bodhi mind weakens, the world
of conflict arises.

When we start sesshin and daily zazen schedule again,
the disputatious mind melts away. This is a concrete example
of the merit of zazen, one we can see. The true, great merit
of zazen is, needless to say, beyond our perception.

*That which is associated with perceptions cannot be the stan-
dard of enlightenment because deluded human sentiment cannot
reach the standard of enlightenment.*

Moreover, although both mind and object appear and disap-

pear within stillness, because this takes place in the realm of self-receiving and self-employing (jijuyu) without moving a speck of dust or destroying a single form, extensive buddha work and profound, subtle buddha influence are carried out.

Something we can perceive cannot be the principle of enlightenment.

Dōgen Zenji's zazen is not for the purpose of making deluded persons into enlightened ones as a sort of conventional Buddhism advocates. True Buddhism is difficult to understand on this point.

In *Gakudō Yojinshū* Dōgen Zenji also said, "A practitioner should not practice buddha-dharma for his own sake, to gain fame and profit, to attain good results, or to pursue miraculous power. Practice only for the sake of the buddha-dharma." This is the difficult point of Dōgen Zenji's zazen. Shakyamuni Buddha questioned his own life and practiced zazen and attained enlightenment. It is the same in the case of Dōgen Zenji. The buddha-dharma lies in the background or as the foundation of zazen, and one's own life lies as the foundation of the buddha-dharma. This is the important point.

Therefore, we study buddha-dharma on the basis of our own lives, and we practice zazen on the basis of the buddha-dharma. Having this attitude is a crucial matter, for in many cases people do not think of their own lives; therefore they cannot understand the buddha-dharma, and in the end, even if they practice zazen, they deviate from genuine zazen.

Since all human beings are alive, each one of us has our own life, and in thinking about our own life each of us has our own outlook or attitude toward life. Yet many people do not truly look at their own lives.

With the example of the cup again, we take it for granted that all of us see the same cup, but it is not true. Each and every one of us sees this cup with our own eyes, from our own angle, through our own way of thinking.

Someone may think that they are lucky to be able to eat lunch today for 1,000 yen, while someone else may think

1,000 yen is too little even for lunch. Some are satisfied with 100,000 yen a month as a salary; others may complain it is too little.

In reality, everything is different without exception, each one of us is living out our own unique life.

Some think this is a good world as it is; others ask themselves why they must live in such a terrible world. Even within a single person, actual feelings are always changing moment by moment.

However, we usually think we see the same cup. We think we are spending money that has the same value. We assume we are living together as members within the same world. This is reification of abstract concepts. When we think of how we should live, we only consider how to spend our lifetime in this world we share. This is merely a technique for living without trouble. Although each of us thinks of our own life and has our own view of life, we only think of various techniques for social climbing. Only a few people really think of their own life as it is.

Although I repeat this many times, it is very difficult to understand. But it is really essential, so please listen again and again. If you listen to it more than a million times, you may finally be convinced and believe it must be so.

One example is the transplanting of Western civilization in Japan. In the Ashikaga (Muromachi) era (1392–1573), guns were introduced by Portuguese who were cast away on Tanegashima Island in the south of Japan. Japanese could use guns as soon as they arrived, but four hundred years later, at the end of the Tokugawa era, their use had been abandoned. In the nineteenth century Westerners came by steamship to Japan with many soldiers armed with much better guns and powerful artillery. In the background of this modernized army was modern Western civilization. Unless we studied modernized society itself, it would be impossible to create a scientific, organized army able to employ such military strength. First of all, we had to accomplish an industrial revolution and attain economic power. In order to do that an educational system had to be established, and the feudalistic system of social rank had to be abolished, lest Japan become a colony of a Western country, conquered by overwhelming military power.

Since India and countries in Southeast Asia failed to study Western civilization, they became colonies of Western countries. The same thing happened in China, too. But Japan studied Western civilization desperately and tried to modernize from within the country. It is said that this is the reason Japan was able to avoid becoming a colony. I read this in Arnold Toynbee's history book.

In the same manner, when we study the buddha-dharma, to study Buddhist terminology is not nearly enough. We should study life itself, which exists as the foundation of Buddhism. We never actually live within the common society we create through reifying abstract concepts, as we usually believe. We should truly believe that each and every one of us, whether we think so or not, is living out the self that is only the self, and we must thoroughly become a person living out the self that is only the self or we cannot embody the genuine buddha-dharma.

When you clearly understand that this world you see is really the world of the self only, and that when you die you die with this whole world, the conventional system of values will disappear.

We think that to be born means to make an entrance into the common society, to live means to compete with others for existence in the common society, and to die means to make one's exit from this society. All people firmly believe in this kind of outlook toward life, but it is not true. Common society does not exist at all. Everyone is born with the world of the self only, lives out life with the original life force of the self that is only the self, and dies with the whole world.

This is an extraordinary idea from the common point of view. You cannot understand it easily, but it is true. As a matter of fact, whether you understand it or not, whether you believe so or not, this is reality.

Before I became a monk, I read *Keiteki* by Nishiari Bokusan Zenji again and again. In this commentary to *Shōbōgenzō*, he said that our zazen should be one in which we get a look equally at both enlightenment and delusion. At that time I could not understand enough to get an equal look. Now I understand, since "that which is associated with perception cannot be the standard of enlightenment." In the true zazen, enlightenment is not good, delusion is not bad. We should look equally at both enlightenment and delusion. Our sitting should be like this. We sit as the self of the entirety of myriad dharmas, as Dōgen Zenji said. Sitting as the self that is only the self, we sit within jijuyu zanmai (samadhi of the self). This zazen has no comparison with zazen based on the desire to get satori and feel good, a kind of personal, psychological condition.

Dōgen Zenji said that to sit in such a way is the true way of enlightenment; such zazen itself is enlightenment. Zazen is not a means to gradually attain enlightenment. We sit zazen, which is dropping off body and mind right now, right here. Practice and enlightenment are not something different. We should not separate practice and enlightenment into two. Since zazen is itself enlightenment, there is no way to think that I become enlightened as a result of zazen practice. To sit zazen is to be in the profound sleep of enlightenment. Therefore, to think that I am enlightened is the same as to think that I sleep well within sound sleep. This is sham sleep. When we sleep really well, we cannot think that we sleep well. In the same way, within zazen, we cannot see if we are enlightened or not. Sometimes we feel clear in zazen, sometimes not; certainly we don't feel clear more often than not. In either condition, zazen is zazen. We sit right in that place where we can look at both enlightenment and delusion equally.

Zazen is not like a realm of death without any scenery. It is untrue that we attain a mental condition of no-thought and no-imagination in zazen. Many and various kinds of thoughts come in and go away. Sometimes we think of food during sitting; we may think of the opposite sex; we usually have fantasies or delusions. However, even if we think of women or food, those are merely the scenery of zazen.

This is the meaning of "both mind and object appear and disappear within stillness."

Here, mind means the six sense organs (eye, ear, nose, tongue, tactile body, and mind), which are the subjects that perceive. Then there are six objects (color and shape, sound, odor, taste, tactile objects, and mental objects) that are perceived. Even within zazen there is various scenery, comings and goings of subjects that see and things seen.

Although there is scenery, this takes place within the whole world sitting in jijuyu zanmai, in which the self is only the self. Since this is scenery inside the world of zazen, it is nothing but enlightenment, appearance and disappearance within enlightenment. To the extent that we are sitting within jijuyu zanmai, there is nothing good, nothing bad. This is the meaning of "without moving a speck of dust or destroying a single form."

This is well explained in the *Keiteki* of Nishiari Zenji: "This should be said as follows. Although there are both subjects and objects which are appearing and disappearing, since this is the realm of jijuyu (self receiving and using), all of them equally become enlightenment. They neither move the slightest bit of dust nor break any single form."

In other words, in the stillness (when we are sitting zazen) various kinds of thoughts arise and go away when we let them go. They disappear, and only the wall remains in front of our eyes. We should be grateful to zazen, which teaches us that all kinds of thoughts fall off when we open our hands, and only the wall is left. We should understand this thoroughly. If we continuously practice, we will understand that various thoughts appearing in our mind are nothing but secretions of our brain.

I don't say thoughts are valueless because they are only secretions. The stomach secretes gastric juice, and the gastric juice digests the food we eat. It is necessary. However, if we eat too much delicious food every day, according to medical books, it causes gastric hyperacidity and might lead to a stomach ulcer or cancer. Also, as a result of too much nutrition, we may get diabetes or heart disease. It's best to remain natural. It's most healthy to leave secretions secreting as secretion.

It is the same in the case of secretions from our brain. Our brain secretes various thoughts. We just keep letting go of them. This is most sound. Firmly grasping our thoughts in the brain or negating them are both no good. Just be natural. See secretion as secretion. Thoughts coming up in our brain are merely scenery. It's no good to chase after them. If you chase them, you are enmeshed in thinking. No chasing after; no throwing away. This is the most important point of zazen.

At that time, nothing "moves a speck of dust or destroys a single form," and everything becomes scenery in the whole world of zazen.

No success or failure exists there. We cannot judge one thing as good and another thing as bad; everything is all right as it is. Both appearing and disappearing are the reality of myriad dharmas.

"Extensive buddha work and profound subtle buddha influence are carried out." We see enlightenment and delusion equally as they are. There is no success or failure. This is true merit.

In the New Testament we read, "He makes His sun rise on the evil and the good, and He pours rain upon the just and the unjust" (Matthew 5:45). True merit is like this. The sun does not distinguish between people. God makes the sun rise on both the good and the evil, and pours rain equally upon all people.

People wear diamond rings on their fingers and think that the fingers feel happy, but actually it is best to wear nothing on the fingers. Fingers feel happy when they forget themselves. Usually we do not use the little finger, but once a little finger is injured, we are very conscious of the finger.

In the same manner, it is not necessarily good for a stomach to eat a lot of delicious food. When we have delicious food, we are apt to eat too much, and the food lies heavily in the stomach. We are conscious of the stomach, and this is certainly not good. It is best to forget the existence of the stomach.

A student preparing for an entrance examination wants to pass; no one wants to fail. Yet the world in which there is no success or failure is the best. We cannot expect such a world in Japan today. It is possible only in the world of zazen. However, there is a group of people who try to put pass and fail into the world of zazen through satori. If you attain satori you succeed, if not you fail. This attitude has nothing to do with the buddha-dharma; it is samsara.

We only have to sit with the self that is only the self, without comparing it to others. It is not necessary at all to visit a Zen master to ask if one is enlightened or not. That is really a stupid question. First of all, to practice the buddha-dharma is to live out the self that is only the self. The truth is that one always has to live out the self that is only the self in any situation, so it is impossible to bring up the question of whether one succeeds or fails.

The grass, trees, and earth affected by this functioning radiate great brilliance together and endlessly expound the deep, wondrous dharma.

The grass, trees, and the land, all things in Nature itself, are the reality of life that is at peace and ease beyond discrimination. To radiate a great light means to be at peace and ease within the self that is only the self.

There are some human beings who become neurotic and have a warped mind; they become timid when they are treated harshly in the world of success and failure. When we practice zazen we are at peace and ease, as the self that is only the self is beyond success and failure. Then we radiate a great light and express the profound and wondrous dharma.

Grasses and trees, fences and walls demonstrate and exalt it for the sake of living beings, both ordinary and sage, and in turn, living beings, both ordinary and sage, express and unfold it for the sake of grasses and trees, fences and walls.

When we sit in zazen facing the trunk of a tree or a wall, even though delusions arise, once we go back to zazen and let go of thoughts, the illusions disappear. Only the tree or the wall remains.

When I was a kid, at the end of the Taisho era or the beginning of the Shōwa era (around the 1920s), there was a person who walked around Tokyo playing the mandolin and begging for money. He wore a cloth on his shoulder on which was the message, "Look up at the sky once a day." Although I was a kid, I thought it was romantic to look up at the sky once a day. But I myself did not look up.

However, when I lived in Ogaki after retiring from Antaiji, I became interested in watching the sky. After I moved to Uji city, I began to take a walk every day for one or one-and-a-half hours on the bank of the Uji River, choosing paths where no cars run. I feel very good when I walk looking up at the sky.

The sky is something wondrous. There is no pattern; it is the same as a wall. Each cloud has a different form. Only when I look up at the sky does it preach that there is a world in which we do not need to be excited. The sky expounds and exalts this for living beings, and that which makes nature the buddha-dharma is zazen. Therefore, living beings expound and exalt this for grass, trees, and fences.

The realm of self-awakening and awakening others is fundamentally endowed with the quality of enlightenment lacking nothing, and allows the standard of enlightenment to be actualized ceaselessly.

Since zazen is jijuyu zanmai, all the myriad dharmas lie within the self. Therefore, the self allows everything to become enlightened, and everything allows the self to be enlightened. This is true self-awakening and awakening of others.

The enlightenment of jijuyu zanmai lacks not even a speck of dust. The standard of enlightenment never ceases to be actualized.

Therefore, even if only one person sits for a short time, because this zazen is one with all existence and completely permeates all time, it performs everlasting buddha guidance within the inexhaustible dharma world in the past, present, and future.

I live with the whole universe in which I am living. Whether I improve or backslide depends only on me. Wherever I go, I am the self that is only the self. When one understands this thoroughly, naturally one will have an aspiration to improve without fail. This is original life force. One puts one's whole energy into this practice right now, right here. "When one accomplishes one thing, one penetrates one thing. When one encounters one practice, one cultivates one practice" (*Genjōkōan*).

Although I have many disciples, I think it strange that an undependable person like me has so many disciples. I do not have any intention to teach my disciples, because people who come to a poor temple like Antaiji to practice and become monks must have within themselves their own aspiration to practice. I don't need to worry about teaching them.

No matter how unreliable I am, there is the wonderful practice of zazen as a community of practitioners at Antaiji. The zazen that each one of us practices is the true teacher. The only thing I should teach my disciples is that zazen is their true teacher. Then each one of them develops without my guidance.

I make them thoroughly aware of the fact that to grow or fall only depends upon the self, and then I allow them to practice with their own aspiration. They cannot refrain from practice of their own accord. I suppose the reason that Dōgen Zenji described the merit of zazen in *Bendōwa* is the same.

Since I thought that way, I completely stopped using the *kyōsaku* (hitting staff) during sesshin at Antaiji. There are some priests who think that they cannot practice zazen without someone hitting their shoulder with a *kyōsaku*. It is not true. It may be good to hit practitioners who only come to sit for one period once in a while. Awakening them by hitting is merit for them in such cases. However, at Antaiji we sit all day long. No matter how sleepy you may be, you cannot sleep fifteen or sixteen hours a day. Once you have slept as long as needed, you naturally awaken. When you awaken you sit zazen wholeheartedly, since it is your own practice.

This is not only relative to the *kyōsaku*. In ordinary society, for example at a company, a boss is always concerned about whether his employees do something bad or not, whether they work hard or not, and how he can oversee them. At schools, teachers keep on the lookout for their students. The buds of youth will be nipped by this attitude.

Each person works to do good for a company or studies to improve himself. We should trust in people's motivation; that is their original life force. Then everyone should try to do their best in things they are good at. A boss or a teacher should only watch over people. My fundamental attitude toward my disciples is not overseeing, but watching over.

Even one period of zazen of a single person, if it is practiced mindfully, is one with all things and completely permeates all time. It is essential to sit with an attitude of being one with the whole world in which the self is living.

If you maintain this attitude, you perform everlasting buddha function within this inexhaustible dharma universe in the past, present, and future. Even one person's zazen has immeasurable influence.

[Zazen] is equally the same practice and the same enlightenment for both the person sitting and for all dharmas. The melodious sound continues to resonate as it echoes, not only during sitting practice, but before and after striking sunyata, *which continues endlessly before and after a hammer hits it. Not only that, but all things are endowed with original practice within the original face, which is impossible to measure.*

When each one of us practices right now, right here as

the self that is only the self, that zazen is the equal and same practice.

Not only in zazen, but when a bell is struck, the melodious sound lasts for a while. Thus the merit of zazen appears within all aspects of the life of the zazen person. One should live to revere zazen as a most venerable buddha, being watched over by zazen and led by zazen. Zazen is not only when we sit on a *zafu* (cushion).

For a true practitioner, there should be no gap between outward appearance and reality. Yet religionists often pretend to be holy persons in front of their believers. Eventually a gap arises between actuality and outward appearance. I believe that if even a slight gap arises, one cannot be a person of living religion.

This is especially important for a person who practices zazen as the self that is only the self. To practice zazen is to practice the reality of the self. If reality and outside appearance are different, the person's practice is no good at all. We should strictly live out the reality of the self and be like the melodious sound made by striking *sunyata*, continuing endlessly.

There is no success and failure in the reality of the self. Just be as it is. We are totally liberated. The self that is only the self is itself absolute enlightenment, and yet as the original life force, it possesses original practice in its original face. Just be the original life force and keep going on to purify yourself endlessly within the life force. This is true practice.

When we practice the reality of the self that is absolute enlightenment to the end, enlightenment and practice cannot be separate. Since we practice based on enlightenment, it is called practice of enlightenment. Practice and enlightenment are one. Therefore, it cannot be measured or grasped. Sawaki Roshi expressed this using the word *yūsui* (profound). The profundity of practice, purifying oneself in the limitless reality of life motivated by original life force, is truly immeasurable. It is really *yūsui*.

You should know that even if all the buddhas in the ten directions, as numerous as the sands of the Ganges River, together engage the full power of their buddha wisdom, they could never reach the limit, or measure or comprehend the virtue, of one person's zazen.

It is said that there are as many buddhas as the grains of sand of the Ganges. When people practice zazen they are all buddhas. Since Shakyamuni Buddha, some twenty centuries have passed. During this period, the number of people who practiced zazen is immeasurable. Even if those immeasurable numbers of buddhas tried to measure the merit of zazen by using computers, it would not be possible.

Part Two

RECITING SUTRAS IS LIKE FROGS IN THE SPRING RICE PADDY, CROAKING ALL DAY AND NIGHT.

In the previous section, Dōgen Zenji described the merit of zazen as jijuyu zanmai. In this part there are eighteen questions and answers to enable us to more clearly understand this.

QUESTION ONE:
Now we have heard that the virtue of this zazen is immense. Stupid people may question this asking, "There are many gates to the buddha-dharma. Why do you only recommend zazen?"

In the beginning of *Bendōwa*, Dōgen Zenji said that burning incense, bowing, nembutsu, repentance, and sutra reading are not necessary, and in another section he emphatically described the limitless virtue of zazen. However, there are various kinds of practice in Buddhism, including offering incense and prostrating oneself in front of a buddha statue, chanting nembutsu, reciting sutras, many sorts of contemplation, meditation, or visualization, the practice of giving, the practice of patience, and so on. It is said that since we human beings have 84,000 desires, there are the

same number of practices (dharma gates) to become free
from each desire. Why did Dōgen Zenji exclusively recommend the practice of zazen?

His answer was:

Because this is the true gate to buddha-dharma.

I suppose, on hearing this kind of answer, there were
people in ancient times who were convinced and said, "You
have won me over." However, in these days, how do people
react when they are told, "Practice zazen! Zazen is the true
gate to buddha-dharma"?

Since ancient people believed that the buddha-dharma
was venerable, saying that zazen is the true gate to buddha-
dharma could work. But people in modern times don't
accept this. Buddhist priests must understand this clearly.
Priests in the Sōtō school often merely repeat, "Buddha-
dharma is such and such," "The buddha way is such and
such," and the audience stifles a yawn. Moreover, they don't
go to listen to such tedious preaching. So in these days, an
answer that says zazen is the true gate to buddha-dharma is
not effective. How shall we answer? I'd like to say that zazen
is the true gate to the life of the self.

There must be people who don't like zazen. Such people look for something that can be a substitute for zazen. For
example, you have a girlfriend and you want to marry her,
but your parents and relatives do not agree. Then you think
of eloping with her. In such a situation, first of all, do not
carry it out right away. Wait quietly for a while. Waiting is a
substitute for zazen. Take your time; then you will naturally
calm down. Suppose you wait for ten or twenty years. No
matter how beautiful and attractive she may be, she will certainly become a withered old woman. It is the same when
you want to fight with someone. Even when you get mad, do
not shake your fist immediately. Wait without an action for a
while, and imagine that you wait for ten years, twenty years,
or until after your death. I don't say you should not fight.
Do it when you really get angry. Or if you love someone, it
is good to get married. However, you will have trouble if you

hit a person immediately and thoughtlessly. And it is no good if you met a woman yesterday and fell in love, then elope with her today and commit joint suicide tomorrow.

A person in his dream found a wallet in the winter night. Since it was frozen, he tried to melt the ice with piss. When he was picking up the wallet, he woke up from the dream and found that he had wet the bed. We ordinary human beings are apt to be lured by illusion and act on that basis, often shooting at the wrong mark. In other words, usually we divide time into small periods, and within the periods we do meaningless things such as fighting with others, coveting things, or bearing a grudge against someone. We create karma within excitement or delusion, and consequently we become involved in the realm of desire, karma, and suffering. Thought is illusion, action is reality, result is an apparition.

Though various thoughts arise within zazen, thoughts are merely secretions. When we let go of thought and act on the basis of reality, we calm down from our excitement. So it is good for people who don't practice zazen to do something only after thinking about it for a long time. If you don't pause a long time, it is important that you do things while you are watched by zazen. In this sense, zazen is the true gate of our own life, the gate to seeing life with the eye of awakening.

QUESTION TWO:
Why is this alone the true gate?

REPLY:
Great Teacher Shakyamuni correctly transmitted the wondrous method for attaining the Way, and the tathagatas of the three times (past, present, and future) also all attain the Way through zazen. For this reason, [zazen] has been conveyed from one person to another as the true gate. Not only that, but all the ancestors of India and China attained the Way through zazen. Therefore, I am now showing the true gate to human and celestial beings.

After quite a long experience of practicing zazen, I now think that our brain has some curious relation with the zazen posture of sitting cross-legged and keeping the spine upright. I don't know why, but I see it through my own experience. When we sit in this posture we feel our abdomen resting comfortably on our crossed legs, and we naturally breathe abdominally. The diaphragm goes down and air gets deep into the *hara*. This posture is wondrous, but you cannot understand it unless you really sit. I believe this is a point of great culture, discovered through Asian religions.

Mankind has invented many things in the past, such as television, the automobile, jet airplanes, rockets, and computers. Though there are many things, they are all meaningless. Why? Because none of them has made human beings noble. However, zazen makes human beings noble. Zazen allows human beings to find the true self. In this sense, zazen is really "the wondrous method for attaining the Way."

The self is born with the world of the self, lives within the world of the self, and dies with the world of the self. Although this is entirely different from the commonsense view, if you sit, you will see that this is reality.

Since Shakyamuni understood this thoroughly through the practice of zazen, he transmitted this reality as the buddha-dharma. Had he not practiced zazen, he wouldn't have realized this reality of the world.

QUESTION THREE:

Relying on either the correct transmitting of the wondrous method of tathagatas or following the tracks of the ancestral teachers is truly beyond our ordinary thinking. However, reading sutras or chanting nembutsu naturally can become a cause of satori. How can just sitting vainly without doing anything be a means for attaining enlightenment?

The meaning of the third question is: Okay. Zazen is good. I understand that it cannot be reached by ordinary thoughts. But it might be possible to become enlightened through various practices, such as reciting sutras and chanting nembutsu. I feel unsatisfied with only sitting silently. In other words, this questioner thinks that to do something is better than to do nothing.

First of all, people in this world like to play with toys. They always feel something lacking if they have no toys at hand. They amuse themselves by playing within relationship to others. Pianos, cameras, golf, and automobiles are all objects of pleasure for such people. This is easy to understand, but as a matter of fact, working hard, involvement in social climbing, even studying or research activities can be nothing more than playing with toys. Among all the human activities in the world, there is nothing in which we can live out our own life without amusing ourselves with toys. Only sitting zazen is free from self-amusement with toys. This is the point where zazen is wondrous.

This is why Dōgen Zenji replied:

That you now consider the samadhi of the buddhas, the unsurpassed great dharma, as vainly sitting doing nothing, is slandering the Mahayana. This is very deep delusion, as if saying that there is no water even while being in the middle of the great ocean.

This person thinks zazen is vain sitting without doing anything. This is a deluded view. As Dōgen Zenji said, we are "already sitting peacefully in the jijuyu zanmai of the buddhas." To practice true zazen is to live being awakened to the reality of the life of the self in its true sense, without playing with toys, without comparison to others, without self-deception or self-amusement. Dōgen Zenji's zazen is the only way to straightforwardly live out the reality of the life of the self that is beyond relation to others. We must understand this thoroughly. There is no way to help you if you say you feel something lacking in zazen.

Doesn't this manifest extensive virtue? It is pitiful that your eyes are not yet open and your mind is still drunk. On the whole, the buddha realm is incomprehensible.

What the buddha-dharma teaches is really incomprehensible. Other religions or philosophies only consider that the mind is the master of the self, and this master owns life. They imagine a society in which we can communicate with each other through intellect, and they throw themselves into the society and believe that they live therein. This is the world of concepts. They think to be born is to enter this world and to die is to get out of this world.

However, reality is the opposite. Life owns the intellect. Therefore intellect never understands life. Today's scientists try to know everything about life, but actually they only know a piece of sand on a beach of limitless life. They may know one hundred pieces of sand in the future. Compared to the infinite, one and one hundred are not different at all. The important thing is to know the infinite. The only important thing for the human intellect to understand is that we cannot understand truth by intellect.

I had a hard time for seven or eight years after I began to practice with Sawaki Roshi, because I could not understand what the buddha-dharma is. In the ninth year, I heard Sawaki Roshi say, "The buddha-dharma is limitless and infinite. It cannot be that which satisfies your desire." These words allowed me to penetrate into buddha's teaching.

Truly, the buddha-dharma is limitless; it cannot be measured or grasped. It is wondrous, and yet we try to understand it through our intellects by every means possible. But that which is infinite and wondrous is not something that satisfies our desire to grasp things. Something infinite cannot be put into something finite.

Usually we think something infinite is the opposite of something finite. This is easy to understand on the surface. There is something infinite, and something finite; if it's not finite, it must be infinite. But if this is so, there is a boundary between finite and infinite, and infinite therefore has a limit and cannot be truly infinite.

Muryō muhen (limitless infinity) in the buddha-dharma is not such a limited infinity. It transcends the boundary between finite and infinite. This is not easy to understand. Even if you try to understand through your intellect, it's impossible. Only when we let go of our thoughts is there infinity.

It is the same in the case of delusion and enlightenment. It is easy to understand that delusion is not good, enlightenment is good. But this is not really the case. True enlightenment cannot be measured by our intellect because it is seeing both enlightenment and delusion equally in one view. "Discriminating mind cannot reach it." Zazen is never merely vain sitting. We are sitting stably in the jijuyu zanmai of the buddhas. This is the true zazen taught by Dōgen Zenji.

We have to be careful about understanding what buddha means. When we hear the word *buddha*, we thoughtlessly imagine some venerable buddhas outside of ourselves and, consequently, we think that the buddha-dharma is about someone else.

Japanese people are not good on this point. For example, right after World War II people thought democracy was something absolutely good. When the word *democracy* was used, they stopped thinking. Before the war, people stopped thinking when they heard the word *emperor*. In the same manner, at the time of Dōgen Zenji, since Buddhism was pretty popular and had authority, it seems that people stopped thinking when they heard the word *buddha*. Without considering why, they thought buddhas were something venerable.

But these days, when people hear the word *buddhas*, instead of worshipping them they say, "So what?" People don't worship the emperor anymore, and democracy still has some power, though it is also fading. From now on, we should be free from all taboos and question everything, "So what?"

These days the word *buddha* sounds like something abstract and unfamiliar. It doesn't work in this modern age. In my words, *buddha* means "life."

Now I am living, breathing, and speaking like this. It's raining outside. When spring comes, trees and grass in the garden at this temple will have buds. This is the function of the one life force.

Not only for living beings, but this life force also enables a jet airplane to fly. We human beings think that we produce cars or jet planes. However, the most essential energy that makes them move is not created by human thought; it is the life force of great nature. Recently an American interplanetary rocket went to Jupiter and Saturn. That was possible because of the same life force. Moreover, planets such as Jupiter or Saturn are revolving around the sun because of the same force. There are billions of galactic systems, and those are also manifestations of the one life force. I call this one force "life."

Zazen is called buddha's jijuyu zanmai. Sitting is life (i.e., buddha) just doing life. Jijuyu zanmai is life living life itself.

In zazen, life, which enables clouds, snow, and rain to manifest as they are, is just sitting. The universe and everything in heaven and earth are all connected to each other within life. This life is "sitting peacefully in the jijuyu zanmai of the buddha." Life is just doing life. "Doesn't this manifest extensive virtue?"

Buddhas are nothing but true life, which enables us to live. However, since we try to grasp it with our small, individual thoughts, we lose sight of it. This is what is meant by "your eyes are not yet open, and your mind is still drunk." It is more difficult to understand that actually individual thinking is also life.

"On the whole, the buddha realm is incomprehensible, unreachable through discrimination." The discriminating mind is *shin shiki*, which is an abbreviation of *shin i shiki*. *Shin* (mind) is *citta* in Sanskrit. *Citta* literally means the power to come together and arise. Our individual lives arise when all different materials gather together. Then we have some power to do things.

I (ego consciousness) is *manas* in Sanskrit. This is the capability to grasp the shin (mind) as "I" and arouse desires to satisfy oneself.

When we reflect on ourselves, we see that we always create action out of the desire to satisfy ourselves. Even when a woman cries pathetically and says that something is completely her fault, by crying in such a way, she is actually trying to satisfy her sentiments. This desire for self-satisfaction is the basis for all human action. It is the core of the subjective or self-centered way of viewing things.

Shiki (consciousness) is *vijnana* in Sanskrit. This means to analyze and separate things, and its function is to analyze objects and understand them.

Shin i shiki (citta, manas, vijnana) is a Buddhist technical term. In our colloquial language this is the function of analyzing things and recognizing them in order to deal with them on the basis of one's desire for self-satisfaction. This enables human beings to survive as living beings. Our human life has the power to grasp all things encountered in life and deal with them for fulfilling our self-centered desire.

In the case of grass or trees, branches do not fight each other even when they are bunched together and don't have enough space to grow. Human beings would surely begin to fight in such a situation, but plants don't. They find their portion, sharing sunlight and air circulation. This is because plants don't have *shin i shiki.*

However, we human beings start conflict with each other because we egocentrically discriminate. Since no one knows when we begin such egocentric discrimination, it is called *mumyo* (ignorance, literally no light) in Buddhism. In Christianity, it is called original sin because separation based on egocentricity is the source of all evil sins. When Adam and Eve ate the forbidden fruit, they had to hide their privates because of a sense of shame. This hiding shows the presence of a wall separating the self from others. We find individual ego there.

This egocentric mind acts as the villain in the play called ignorance or original sin. But from a broader perspective, since the play becomes entertaining because of the villain, we don't need to really hate the villain. We should view discrimination in this manner.

However, we should simply realize that the discriminating mind may have the ability to solve all problems in life, but it cannot handle the problem of dying. Many people think that life is only living. This is not true. Life includes living and dying. Discriminating mind is called the subject in human psychology. In the West, "reason" is not subjective, but only has the ability to view things objectively. But reason also is a subject, as a general concept that has been abstracted from the subjective view common to many human beings.

We usually think in a very egocentric way, with our thoughts expressed in words. When we have a certain image, we capture it in a word and understand it as such. This is called *logos* (concept). Using *logos* as a medium, we communicate with each other and create a world in which people understand each other. This is our society.

Consequently, in human society, each member thinks the self is central. But this self is considered to be common to any person, you or me. We create a general concept of "self" that forms the foundation for rational thinking. The world of scientific study has developed through human efforts to find a logical way of thinking that can be understood by all people. This human effort toward study has resulted in modern natural science or technological civilization. Scientists think according to logic based not on individual discriminative views or personal preferences but on discrimination based on general concepts held by human beings. Scientists see things with the general self of general subjects, or the way of viewing things that is common in all human beings. This method of study enables us to send a rocket to Jupiter or Saturn and have it send real-time pictures to the earth. Then has the problem of human death been resolved by this development of a scientific civilization? Absolutely not! Perhaps it may become possible in the future to handle all problems within life through scientific technology, but the problem of death cannot be solved.

Subsistence and life are different. Subsistence is limited to being alive. But life is born, lives, and dies. Reason or technology cannot even touch it. It is really "unreachable through discrimination."

Much less can it be known with no faith and inferior insight.

According to Buddhist definition, to have faith means to be pure and clear. True life connected with myriad dharmas, instead of individual, physiological life, becomes pure and clear as the life of the self. This is faith. This life of the self is easily tainted due to the power of the personal egocentric mind. Letting go of thoughts, we become pure and clear as true life. This is called *namu* or *kimyo* (to take refuge). *Kimyo* means "to return to a life that completely permeates into everything, everywhere."

Often we say "I believe in God" or "I believe in Buddha." This is the faith based on the understanding that our thoughts can never touch life. However, it is very difficult for us common people to understand this. We think that since we can handle living through thought, we can also solve the matter of life that includes life and death by the same means.

Many well-educated Japanese proudly say that they don't believe in religion. This is the same as saying that they are foolish. Those people only seek an upper-class livelihood, money, power, and fame. I have heard that primitive people in Papua New Guinea count only one and two. They say "many" when they have more than two. In the same manner, the Japanese only know material life and money; they are really primitive. People like this are people "with no faith and inferior insight."

Only people of great capacity and true faith are able to enter.

Thus completely understanding that the discriminating mind does not reach life, one lets go of thought. This is true faith.

People without faith have difficulty accepting, even when taught. Even at Vulture Peak, there was a group of people of whom Buddha said, "It is good that they leave."

We cannot do anything for people who only pursue materially abundant life and money. When Shakyamuni was preaching the Lotus Sutra at Vulture Peak, *shravakas* and *pratyeka* buddhas, who grasped Buddha's teaching as a particular doctrine, thought Shakyamuni was teaching something different from and beyond their own understanding since the Lotus Sutra expresses that the true form of all dharma is beyond our thought. Therefore they considered it worthless to listen and wanted to leave. Three thousand people stood up and left. At the time Shakyamuni said, "It is good that they leave." He didn't ask them to stay.

Generally, if true faith arises in your heart, you should practice and study.

I wrote essays for a series on Sawaki Roshi's sayings for the Asahi newspaper, later published as the book *Yadonashi Kōdō Hokkusan.* [An English translation of the book was published by Kyoto Sōtō Zen Center in 1991 entitled *Zen Teaching of "Homeless" Kōdō.*] I tried to explain buddha-dharma in a very understandable style using colloquial language and examples from modern society. However, I heard that many people complained that it was difficult. I think those people could not understand because they never thought of the problem of one's own life that includes life and death; they never remembered that they will die sooner or later. The problem of our life begins when we see that we are unavoidably aging and have to die. Our life includes life and death, but people do not recognize it.

When I talk about death, people say, "I don't want to discuss such an inauspicious matter." They have no sense for hearing buddha-dharma. But they must be good in the struggle for existence. I know of an example of such a person. He worked for a big company and became a section chief. After retirement he started a business by himself and was so successful that he finally owned two companies. As he aged he was stricken with paralysis, although he used to be a very strong person who could work like blazes without ever experiencing illness. When he was confined to bed suffering with a fatal disease, he was thrown into despair. His doctor said that if he didn't have massage and exercise rehabilita- tion treatment, he would never move again. When he had such treatment or exercise, he cried with pain as if the whole world had broken, and asked them to stop. Consequently, his body went untreated, and he was no longer able to move his arms and legs. Yet since his stomach was strong, he ate meat and chocolate every day. After he had been in bed for seven or eight years, I made a call on him once. He was like a baby, and said with a miserable voice, "Uchiyama-san, it's no good anymore." I felt really sorry for him, but I couldn't find any way to help him.

Living out life is different from the art of competition for survival. If you go through the world with the attitude "I care for livelihood, money, and nothing more, but anyway let's have a baby," you will fall into a pit in the final stage of your life, just like him.

We should think about our own life based on the fact that living beings have to die. First of all we must clarify death, and then we can start to live from that point. In the Jōdō Shin School (one of the Japanese Pure Land Buddhist schools), they have an important term *goshō* (later life). This doesn't refer to the next life in the pure land after one's death, but to the present life after clarifying death. In fact, we should live vividly in the present life precisely because we are going to die. This is the most beautiful way of life.

Almost all of those who visit Buddhist temples in Japan are aged people. They come to temples to search for the buddha-dharma only when they have to face death. But it's really too late. I'm glad that here we have many young peo- ple, because it is most important to clarify death from the start.

Fundamentally, Western civilization is one of survival. It is concerned with how to live skillfully instead of looking at one's death. Buddhist culture begins from seeing death. For example, in the Buddhist countries in Southeast Asia, people practice at Buddhist monasteries when they are young, and they work in society. When they are aged, they retire from society and enter monasteries again to spend the rest of their lives practicing zazen quietly and seeing their death. I think this is really a wonderful approach to life that is in accord with the rhythm of human life, that is, being born, living, and dying.

I have seen many elderly American women who put on loud lipstick and thick makeup and wear crimson dresses while shopping on the streets in Kyoto. Japanese often praise them, saying that American women are young-looking until their old age. They think the Japanese look old too soon. Of course, it is nice to be youthful in appearance, but too much unnatural makeup only makes people look ugly. What can such people do when they are confined to bed with a fatal sickness? We have to think about this point carefully. We should watch aging and dying, and on that basis we must aspire to live out our true life.

Young people may think that they have a lot of time before aging; it will occur only twenty or thirty years later. However, thirty or forty years pass in a twinkling. I actually feel this when I look back on my life from the present time. Time flies. Life always has death at its side.

Regret not having the blessing of dharma from long ago.

This is the dharma in the expression "One mind is all the dharmas; all the dharmas are one mind." One mind permeates into all living beings; all beings that are permeated by life are one mind.

Usually we think we are born into a society that had already been in existence prior to our birth, and all dharmas form society with the self as one member within society. Therefore, we assume the self is one out of all the numerous existences. We feel upset and suffer from loneliness because we think we are one in the world in which numerous people are living. So we try to go to places where many people gather and do things with other people in order to become free from loneliness. This is a human action called massing.

After we lost World War II, many new religions—such as Sōka Gakkai and Tenrikyō—became popular in Japan, I believe due to this same phenomenon. In 1950 or 1951, while I was staying at Antaiji in Kyoto, I read a book about Tenrikyō because an old lady in our neighborhood asked me to read it. The book was very shallow and not interesting at all, but since the lady urged me to go to a festival in Tenri, I accompanied her. I was surprised. The huge shrine hall was crammed with people, and after a while the *mahashira-san* (the head of the religion) appeared and delivered a worn-out sermon on "the human mind is something warm." Almost all the believers were sleeping in their seats while he was preaching. It seems that when the same sort of people gather they feel secure and drop into a doze.

Sawaki Roshi once said, "If you are satisfied by Tenrikyō, go to Tenrikyō. If you like Sōka Gakkai, join Sōka Gakkai. No matter how many followers they have, coal cinders are only coal cinders."

Those people consider themselves only one out of all. It is worthless for numerous people to gather if they remain only a collection of individuals, one out of all.

We should see ourselves from a different perspective. It is true that we are living as one out of all, but we are also the self that is all of all. All beings exist only within our life experience. We are living only within our experience of the world. Our self is living and dying with all beings, so the content of our self is immeasurably abundant. We don't see the reality of our life if we only see the self that is born alone in society, and leaves alone. Dōgen Zenji said that people who believe in such a way don't have "the blessing of dharma."

Furthermore, do you really know the virtue to be gained by working at such practices as reading sutras or chanting nembutsu? The notion that merely making sounds by moving your tongue leads to the virtue of the buddha work is completely meaningless.

Dōgen Zenji's pen is becoming more and more vitriolic

here. I used to think Buddhist monks must chant sutras, but since I read this comment by Dōgen Zenji I have stopped chanting them.

It is extremely far, tremendously distant, from resembling buddha-dharma. Also, as for opening the sutras, if you clearly understand what Buddha has taught as the principle of sudden and gradual practice, and practice in accord with that teaching, you will certainly accomplish enlightenment. Vainly wasting your thinking and discrimination does not compare to the virtue of gaining bodhi.

Sutras are like a statement on the virtues of a medicine. It says that you should take a certain amount of the medicine when you have such and such symptoms. If you take the medicine accordingly, it works. It is meaningless to read the statement three times a day.

Sudden practice means you become enlightened suddenly through practice. Gradual practice means you practice and accomplish enlightenment gradually.

In sutras, it is said that practicing zazen is the true way of life. Only reading the sutra [without practice] is worthless.

Studying Buddhism as doctrine is to "waste your thinking and discrimination." There are quite a few *Shōbōgenzō* scholars who never practice zazen. It is of no value to read *Shōbōgenzō* because it is good material on which to write a thesis. Since it says in *Shōbōgenzō* that we should practice zazen, we should practice zazen straightforwardly.

Intending to reach the buddha way through stupid, ceaseless chanting millions of times is like steering a cart north and trying to go south. It is also the same as trying to put a square peg in a round hole. Reading literature while ignoring the way of practice is like a person reading a prescription but forgetting to take the medicine; what is the benefit?

Continuously uttering sounds like frogs in a spring rice paddy croaking day and night is also ultimately worthless.

Furthermore, people deeply blinded by fame and profit have difficulty abandoning these things because their greed is exceed-

ingly deep. Since this was the case in ancient times, why shouldn't it be so in the modern world? We must feel the utmost sympathy.

I know there are many strange things in the world, but the most strange thing to me is that many so-called religious teachers are not really living by their religion. I really become sick seeing many religious leaders think only about how to attract the masses. Some of them make the appeal that if you believe in their religion you will be successful in your business, or you will recover from illness. That is too simple and out of the question. Another kind of religious person thinks that to be religious is to say only fantastic or moralistic things that are admired by the masses. Since many people gather around such religionists, they collect a lot of money and consequently gain fame. Because I always say that you will age and die, not many people come to me.

A long time ago, when I was young, I was a teacher at a Catholic theological school for a while. I thought that the Catholic mass was worthy of collecting people. First of all, the music was glorious. It was wonderful to see bright candles, burning incense, children wearing pretty robes, and the celebrants wearing beautiful garments, offering up prayers, and singing hymns. It was worthwhile to see such a show even if I had to pay. The masses love that kind of ceremony. Ceremonies were one of the important methods for leading and controlling people before mass communication media developed.

Ancient people didn't understand teachings about how to live or what they shouldn't do. It was much more understandable to say God ordered us to do such and such. People accepted it more easily when things were presented as orders from God. Consequently, religion controlled almost all aspects of people's lives through ceremonies such as coming of age, weddings, funerals, and memorials.

For example, in the Old Testament it said that, as an order from God, people should not eat octopus, squid, or sea slugs. I think since the Jewish country was far from the ocean and hot, those things went bad soon, and eating them

caused people to become sick. Since people didn't understand hygienic or medical reasons, they were told it was an
order from God. Also in the Old Testament, the number of
men who could be soldiers and go to war and the number of
sheep had to be registered. Preparation for war and the
national census were under the control of the religious
power. As a residue of such power by religions, even these
days there are various rites of passage and ceremonies.
There is no end to collecting numbers of people, money,
and fame. This is really pitiful.

*You must clearly understand that the wondrous dharma of
the seven buddhas manifests its essential meaning and is received
and upheld only when a practitioner matches the mind, actualizes
awakening, and follows and receives the true transmission of a
master who embodies the Way and clarifies the mind. This [won-
drous dharma] cannot be fully understood by a teacher who only
studies words. Therefore, immediately cease this skepticism, practice the way of zazen under the guidance of a true teacher, and
fully actualize the jijuyu zanmai of the buddhas.*

The wondrous dharma of the seven buddhas means the
genuine buddha-dharma. A master who embodies the Way
and clarifies the mind is very difficult to find. It is not good
that someone who has only a little experience of zazen
teaches zazen to beginners, for there is various scenery in
the practice of zazen, and teachers must be individuals who
have been practicing until they thoroughly experience each
and every scene in zazen. Because life involves human
thought, there is various scenery as life. Sometimes during
zazen we may feel as if we are enlightened to emptiness, but
when we go outside and see beautiful women, we certainly
have delusive desire again.

In my case, I married twice before I became a monk.
Both of my wives died. For a while my mind wasn't moved
by seeing beautiful women, because I remembered my wife's
death face. I thought I was advanced in contemplation of
impermanence, but unfortunately such contemplation of
impermanence is also impermanent. After a while, I began

to feel desire again when I saw young women. Now a long time later, I feel I am much improved, but it only means I am really aged.

All of this is simply the scenery of life. If your enlightenment is bothered by such scenery, it is not true enlightenment.

For example, I heard a story about a certain Rinzai teacher who had already attained so-called enlightenment. One day he took an airplane to some affair. Unfortunately, the airplane rolled badly and the roshi was terribly airsick. This is physiologically only natural. However, the roshi thought that it was no good for an enlightened person like himself to be airsick, and he tried to pretend that he was not. When he got off the airplane he asked his attendant not to tell anyone about his being airsick. It is really inconvenient if an enlightened person cannot get airsick or have a cold. It's too much to ask an attendant not to tell anyone that the roshi has a cold.

In short, it's not true enlightenment if it is obstructed by delusion. It is not reliable unless the enlightenment is always there in whatever situation. As I said before, it is important to see both delusion and enlightenment with one eye. Both delusion and enlightenment are the scenery of life. We should sit on a foundation from which we can view them equally.

Dōgen Zenji's zazen is not that of making delusion into enlightenment, but that of transcending enlightenment and delusion. It is not making an ordinary human being into a sage, but transcending ordinary beings and sages. Common people think that Buddhism is making delusion into enlightenment and an ordinary being into a sage, but this is not in accord with buddha-dharma.

Going beyond both enlightenment and delusion, ordinary beings and sages, a person who sits thoroughly on such a foundation can be called a master who embodies the Way and clarifies the mind. When a practitioner matches the mind, actualizes awakening, and practices with such a teacher, the true buddha-dharma will be succeeded to without fail. A teacher who only studies words, a person who tries to handle buddha's teaching by merely studying texts, cannot understand the core of the buddha-dharma.

TOO MANY TEACHERS DIRECT PEOPLE WITHOUT KNOWING THEIR OWN DIRECTION

QUESTION FOUR:

The Hokke (Tendai) and Kegon teachings, which have been transmitted now in our country, are both the most sublime teachings of the Mahayana. Moreover, the Shingon teaching was intimately transmitted from Vairocana Tathagata to Vajrasattva, from teacher to disciple without deviation. Its principal is that "Mind itself is buddha" or "This mind becomes buddha," which propounds the true awakening of the five buddhas at the instant of sitting, without passing through many kalpas of practice. This must be called the pinnacle of buddha-dharma. In spite of that, what superior features in the practice you are now speaking about cause you to recommend this only and set aside those others?

The Hokke School mentioned here is not today's Nichiren School, but refers to the Tendai School. The main temple of the Kegon School is Tōdaiji in Nara, famous for the Great Buddha. This school did not spread widely; only thirty-odd Kegon temples remain in Japan. The profound philosophies of those two schools are considered to be "the most sublime teachings of Mahayana."

This question was likely to be asked by many Buddhists at the time of Dōgen Zenji, for it seems that the Shingon School was considered the deepest teaching in Buddhism. In the Heian and early Kamakura period in which Dōgen Zenji was active, the Shingon and Tendai Schools were most popular. In particular the esoteric teaching and practice of shingon matched the mystical feeling of the Japanese people.

As Japanese are easily affected by authority or fashion, they unconditionally follow something powerful. In the thirteenth century, everyone thought Buddhism was unquestionably honorable. People just stop thinking and follow authority. Among the various Buddhist schools, Shingon was outstandingly powerful.

Vairocana Tathagata is well known in Japan by the name Dainichi Nyorai. Cosmic reality is symbolized and called by this name. It is the undivided universal power of nature. According to this tradition, Dainichi Nyorai preached about the realm of inward enlightenment, and Kongosatta (Vajrasattva) compiled these teachings and stored them in an iron stupa in South India. Kongosatta is another name for Fugen Bosatsu (Samantabhadra Bodhisattva) in esoteric Buddhism. It is said that hundreds of years later, the iron stupa was opened by Nagarjuna, and the secret teachings of the Kongokai (Vajradhatu, Diamond Realm) and Taizokai (Garbhadhatu, Womb Matrix Realm) began to be transmitted.

Dainichi Nyorai is the force of cosmic nature itself, and human beings are also a product of great nature. Therefore, just as they are, human beings are nothing other than buddha. I am breathing in this way, blood is circulating in my body, and various kinds of thoughts are arising in my mind. Just living is itself a wonderful incident within great nature. The mind (or self) is itself buddha.

It is not strange to say that our life is nothing but buddha. "This mind becomes buddha" means that we become buddha on the basis of mind. All of us are buddhas as we are, without some special practice, but we do not actualize the buddha.

"The true awakening of the five buddhas at the instant of sitting" is an interesting doctrine of the Shingon School. I will explain it briefly.

Our consciousnesses: Eye, ear, nose, tongue, body, i.e., the five senses that cause the five perceptions (sight, hearing, smell, taste, touch), are called the first five consciousnesses. The sixth consciousness is called thought consciousness (*i shiki*, Sanskrit *mano vijnana*); the seventh is *manas* consciousness (*mana shiki*, Sanskrit *manas vijnana*); the eighth is *alaya* consciousness (*alaya shiki*, Sanskrit *alaya vijnana*); and the ninth is undefiled consciousness (*anmara shiki*, Sanskrit *amala vijnana*).

Thought consciousness is the function of thinking various things. Manas consciousness, which grasps individual life force as ego and sees things in an egocentric way, comes out of alaya consciousness. Alaya consciousness is, precisely speaking, individual life force rather than consciousness.

Before I said that mind (*citta*, which means gathering and arising) is thought, which is formed by various factors and wells up. What are the factors? Hereditary transmission from parents, individual circumstances in which we are born and grow up, and the fact of being born in Japan in the twentieth century are all factors that together form our personality. Furthermore, we depend upon today's weather, temperature, and our physical condition. All such factors together enable us to live as individual life forces.

Alaya is this gathering and arising from immeasurable factors. Alaya is also called storehouse consciousness because all of our experiences are stored like seeds in it. Those seeds sprout some time later and cause us to act in certain ways. There are two aspects to our lives. One is that various factors together bring about each thing as a result; another is that we learn through each experience, and we judge and do things based upon what we have learned. This is the meaning of alaya consciousness. So I think alaya is our individual life force.

From the alaya, manas consciousness arises. Mind is nothing but a collection of all the different accidental factors, and yet we grasp thoughts caused by accident, call them "I," and attach ourselves to this. The function of perceiving the individual life force as ego is called manas consciousness. In Yuishiki (the Consciousness-only philosophy of the Yogacara School) it is said that manas consciousness consists of always together with ignorance opposing egolessness (*gachi*, Sanskrit *atoma moha*); a mistaken view of the existence of ego (*gaken*, Sanskrit *atoma drsti*); arrogance based on ego (*gaman*, Sanskrit *atma mana*); and ego attachment (*gaai*, Sanskrit *atoma sneha*). Manas consciousness brings about the discriminating mind called thought consciousness.

Thought consciousness distinguishes one thing from another. It is not neutral distinction, but discriminates based on one's own point of view. We discriminate based on our desire for self-satisfaction. This doctrine of alaya, manas, and thought consciousness means nothing more or less than that we see everything in the world through our desire for self-satisfaction.

In terms of Western psychology, the first five consciousnesses are senses and perceptions; the sixth is usual consciousness. The seventh is so-called self-consciousness, and the eighth is the unconscious or subconscious. In Buddhism, these together are explained as the source of desire for self-satisfaction.

This is the theory of Yuishiki of the Yogacara School. In Shingon teaching a ninth undefiled consciousness is posited. It was the thought that the eighth consciousness is nothing other than the force of great nature, that is, life, which is connected with the whole universe.

Our mind has such a structure and function. When we attain buddhahood, the first five consciousnesses function as wisdom of action (*joshosa chi*, Sanskrit *krtyanusthana jnana*); the sixth functions as wisdom of well observing (*myōkansatsu chi*, Sanskrit *pratyaveksana jnana*); the seventh functions as wisdom of equality (*byodosho chi*, Sanskrit *samata jnana*); the eighth functions as wisdom of the great mirror (*daienkyo chi*, Sanskrit *adarsa jnana*); and the ninth functions as wisdom of the dharma universe (*hokkai taisho chi*, Sanskrit *dharmadhatu svabhava jnana*).

When we attain buddhahood, our senses and perceptions become wisdom that enables us to work for all living beings. Thought consciousness functions as wisdom that thoroughly observes the world and recognizes the various faculties of sentient beings in order that we might teach them and resolve their doubts. Manas consciousness becomes wisdom that observes the equality of everything after denying egocentricity. Alaya consciousness becomes wisdom that reflects all things as clearly as a great mirror. Undefiled consciousness becomes wisdom that is itself the reality of the dharma realm.

The buddha of the wisdom of action is called Fukujōju Nyorai (Sanskrit Amoghasiddhi Tathagata). The buddha of the wisdom of well observing is called Muryōju Nyorai (Sanskrit Amitabha Tathagata). The buddha of the wisdom of equality is called Hosho Nyorai (Sanskrit Ratnasambhava Tathagata). The buddha of the wisdom of the great mirror is called Ashuku Nyorai (Sanskrit Akshobhya Tathagata). The buddha of the wisdom of the dharma universe is called Dainichi Nyorai (Sanskrit Mahavairocana Tathagata). The five buddhas in the *Bendōwa* text are those five buddhas.

"Propounding the true awakening of the five buddhas at the instant of sitting" means that Dainichi Nyorai in the Vajradhatu takes his position at the center. His head is not shaved, but he has long hair, wears a jewel crown that symbolizes the five wisdoms, wears a heavenly robe, and demonstrates the wisdom fist mudra. This is the appearance of Dainichi Nyorai in the Vajradhatu. The buddha embodies the five wisdoms in one sitting.

It is interesting to look at buddha images if you have this sort of knowledge. The teaching of the Shingon School seems interesting and very profound. Consequently, this question arises.

REPLY:

Buddhist practitioners should know not to argue about the superiority or inferiority of teachings and not to discriminate between superficial or profound dharma, but should only know whether the practice is genuine or false.

Each time I read *Shōbōgenzō*, I think that Dōgen Zenji was a very straightforward person; he wrote as outspokenly as he thought. For example, whenever he said, "You should know . . ." in a firm way, he wrote on an important matter after that. This reply is no exception. How important it is to know whether our practice is genuine or false!

As I often say, almost all that we do is playing with toys. Even when we practice zazen, we easily make it into a plaything.

Once I wrote an essay in a magazine, so a photographer visited me to take my photo for the article. I heard that he was not a professional but a very earnest photographer. He held several expensive cameras, changing lenses and using powerful illumination. He directed me to face this way or that way and took several pictures, but when I received the magazine I found that my good-looking face looked very plain and no good at all.

On the other hand, when I published a book of origami (paper-folding), a photographer came and took pictures artlessly with a thumb-marked and flawed camera, but his photos made me look much better than I really am.

Later I read an article about two kinds of photographers, and then I understood the difference. It said that real professional photographers, although of course they use their cameras carefully, take many pictures, so their cameras become dirty and flawed. But they take good pictures. The other kind of photographer is simply a camera maniac. They always polish their cameras. Even among photographers there are two groups. Some really take photos, and others play with cameras as a kind of toy.

There are people who play with zazen as a toy. For example, temple priests spend money to advertise in order to collect people for a zazen group. Such priests are often caught up in thought during sitting, seeing the other people's backs. They may pursue the thought that since so many people come to sit, they should build a magnificent zazen hall, and so they make a plan to build a zendo. Of course, they don't build it with their own money; they wander here and there fund-raising. Since these priests are not really devoted to zazen, it is very natural that the members also do not practice seriously. Consequently, when the priest has collected enough money to build a zazen hall, no one comes to sit. I know many examples like this. Such priests only play with zazen as a toy.

Sawaki Roshi often said, "Shave your head, put on an okesa, and sit. That's all." This saying precisely expresses the nature of zazen as jijuyu zanmai (samadhi of receiving and using self). But if we are not careful, even this statement of Sawaki Roshi becomes a kind of plaything. It is really regrettable.

Some people shave their heads and becomes monks, then they collect and choose materials such as hemp or cotton and are picky about the color of their okesa. This attitude makes the okesa a kind of plaything. When such people practice zazen, they consider rituals such as turning clockwise or counter-clockwise essential. They make zazen a kind of ceremony. Ceremonies are empty forms that have no real content. They simply become authority. Zazen shouldn't be a ceremony, but we should live by zazen. Therefore we do not need to build a zazen hall. Wherever it is quiet we can sit when we have time.

This is what Dōgen Zenji meant when he said, "Buddhist practitioners should know not to argue about the superiority or inferiority of teachings and not to discriminate between superficial or profound dharma, but should only know whether the practice is genuine or false." Not to play with any toy is the most crucial point. We should put our whole body and mind into practice.

In Shingon practice, they make an altar (*zōdan*). *Dan* means mandala. A mandala is a painting in which the inward enlightenment of Dainichi Nyorai, himself the symbol of the dharma universe, is expressed symbolically and contemplated. You may have seen them: many buddhas painted on a large scroll of paper. Mandalas are sometimes exhibited at Tōji in Kyoto or other Shingon temples. I think they are wonderful as Buddhist art, but they are simply toys from the point of view of true practice. No matter how beautifully and sublimely painted, they are merely artistic works after all.

Shingon priests draw a magic boundary that indicates a sacred area, enshrine buddha images, and practice *samaya*, which indicates the equality of buddhas and sentient beings.

I heard from a Shingon priest that when they have ceremonies at big temples, many mandala paintings are hung so that they really feel as if they have entered the world of buddhas. They don't use electric light, but illuminate the paintings with candlelight in order to create a mysterious atmosphere. In such sacred places, they have ceremonies to confer certain status on a disciple by sprinkling water on the disciple's head.

Shingon priests also practice *goma* (wood burning), in which they make a fire with wood so that this fire, symbolizing wisdom, may burn defiled delusion and also protect people from disasters. This practice originated in the ancient Indian religion called fire worship Brahmanism. Shingon followers pray to buddhas or guardian gods by purifying the three karmas (body, speech, and mind) and becoming one with them. Decorating a shrine hall is important in Shingon. They say that faith arises from dignified ornaments. In short, Shingon practice is like this.

I cannot help questioning such a kind of practice. The philosophy is very profound, but in their essential practice they decorate halls with paintings or make a fire, which is nothing other than playing with dolls and fire. For some reason, lofty philosophy has been combined with low-level, superstitious practice. As Dōgen Zenji said, we should not discuss the profundity of teachings, but examine whether the practice is genuine or not. Do not play with toys, but practice the reality of life.

Once I received a letter from an old lady who used to be a geisha. After her parents' death she was adopted by her aunt. When she was fourteen years old she was raped by her stepfather and sold as a geisha. She was redeemed by a rich person when she was twenty-one, and she was happy for a while. However, her husband was a licentious man. When she was in her fifties he brought in a young woman and said, "From today, this woman is my wife. You are a housemaid." At that time she almost became crazy, but a son adopted from relatives had a newborn baby, so she tried to be patient as the baby was her final treasure. But her stepson and his wife left her house with their baby because they thought living with such an immoral family would not be good for their child. She wrote to me that she had nothing to live for and asked me what to do. At the time she was in her sixties. Since I could not find any words to comfort her, I sent her one of my books titled *Gudō* (Way seeking).

She wrote back after a while, and in her second letter she asked about one of my poems in the book. In the poem, whose title is "Mandala," there were the lines

> *In serenity, everything permeates*
> *each other*
> *and becomes a dignified mandala*
> *of the whole world of the self.*
> *It is gratifying to be aging.*

"It is gratifying to be aging" is a bit of an affected expression. The old lady asked me what this phrase meant. Though it's difficult to explain its meaning, I tried to write her using plain language.

It is said that women live on love. I think there are three kinds of love. The first type is sexual love. In our youth we only know this sort of love. The old lady had been smeared with this type of instinctive love.

The second type is like petting and living for grandchildren. This is love that makes a toy of someone or something. A lonely person's love for dogs or cats as pets is this same type of love. This is not true love.

Then what is true love? Each and every one of us is living as the self that is only the self. Everything we encounter in this world is the content of our own world. Therefore we value, take care of, and think tenderly of every one of these things as a part of ourselves. This is the third type, true love.

That is what I meant when I wrote "In serenity, everything permeates each other/ and becomes a dignified mandala/ of the whole world of the self." No matter how skillfully we paint buddha images as art, such a mandala is not reality itself. The universe of the mandala is inside myself; that is the whole world of the self.

When I was young, since I also had strong sexual desire, I was interested in and attached to many different things. I couldn't actually feel such love. But now I am aging, not many outward things weigh on my mind, and sexual desire naturally falls away. When I think of these conditions, I deeply feel that to be aging is wonderful. I hope the old lady understood this.

There were those who flowed into the buddha way drawn by grasses, flowers, mountains, or rivers.

This refers to Reiun Shigon (ninth century; Lingyun Zhiqin in Chinese). For thirty years Reiun had been wandering various districts as a monk seeking the Way. Once he plodded down a mountain and found a small village like a Shangri-la. It was in the spring, and he saw peach blossoms in their glory everywhere. At the instant he saw the flowers his breath was taken away, and he uttered this poem:

> *For thirty years, a person seeking the sword.*
> *How many times have leaves fallen and*
> *branches grown?*
> *After seeing the peach blossoms*
> *Even till now, never a doubt.*

He saw the same scenery many times for thirty years—leaves falling in autumn and branches growing in spring. Once he encountered the scene of peach blossoms in their glory, he really awakened to what he had been seeking. There is certainly this kind of satori.

For example, kids read a love story. They read such novels because they are somehow interested in such stories, but they don't really understand what love toward the opposite sex or the torments of love are like. However, after they arrive at the age of puberty and begin to feel the urge of sex, when they encounter a desirable girl or boy, there certainly is a time when they actually understand what love is all about. Aha, that's it! The reality and knowledge through words hit each other and become one.

"Mountains or rivers" refers to Sotoba (1036–1101; Su Dongpo, a Zen practitioner and great poet). When he stayed at Mount Lushan overnight, he made a poem:

> *The voice of the valley is endlessly*
> *preaching.*
> *The color of the mountain is nothing but*
> *the pure body.*
> *During the night, I heard eighty-four*
> *thousand verses.*
> *How shall I expound this to others?*

The sounds of a valley stream and the scenery of a mountain are all preaching the buddha-dharma that is universal life.

There are some who received and upheld the buddha mudra from grasping earth, stones, sand, or pebbles.

When Shakyamuni was begging for food, a boy playing with sand put a handful of sand into Buddha's iron bowl as if it were rice. Shakyamuni was happy with the boy's offering; he took the sand back to the monastery and added it to the wall mud for the wall in the monastery. In a later life, the boy was reborn as King Ashoka [a great Buddhist devotee and patron]. This story teaches that the wish to offer is important.

Furthermore, words that express the vastness [of reality] are even more abundant than all the myriad things, but also the turning of the great dharma wheel is contained in one speck of dust.

Everything is life as buddha-dharma. Each and every being is expounding buddha-dharma. Even in a tiny speck of dust, buddha-dharma is stored.

Therefore, the words "The mind itself is buddha" are like the moon reflected in the water. The principle "at the instant of sitting becoming buddha" is also a reflection within a mirror. Don't be caught up in the skillfulness of words.

The reality is not in phrases like "the mind itself is buddha" or "becoming buddha in one sitting." Words are like the moon on a drop of water or a reflection in a mirror. The reality is only in the reality itself.

Now, in order to allow you to become an authentic person of the Way, I recommend practice that directly actualizes bodhi, and am showing you the wondrous way that is simply transmitted by buddha ancestors. Also, in transmitting buddha-dharma, you must definitely have as a true teacher someone who accords with enlightenment. It is worthless to take as a guiding teacher a scholar who just makes calculations about words, since this would be like a blind person leading the blind.

Sawaki Roshi often said that Buddhist scholars are just like clerks at a pawnshop. They have a bunch of pawn tickets, and they categorize pawn articles and store them on a certain shelf in a storehouse. They don't handle real things as their own. Yet it is also a mistake to give up using words and letters. There are many Zen teachers who say that buddha-dharma has nothing to do with words or logic. If reason that uses words or logic is not good, they should become vegetables. That is not good either. Having reason and intellect and using words is also the reality of human life. This is the most subtle point in buddha-dharma. Buddha-dharma is not flat; it has a three-dimensional structure. In one aspect, buddha-dharma should be clearly expressed by words. Use reason and words, but then let go of them and decisively settle down into the reality of the self.

However, from ancient times to the present there have been many Zen teachers who instructed people without having settled in the self themselves. We should not have teachers who do not know where they should go, and yet who like to own people and take them here and there.

Now, the followers of the authentic transmission of buddha ancestors all esteem the clear-sighted masters who have attained the way and accord with enlightenment, and request them to maintain buddha-dharma. Because of this, deities from seen and unseen realms who come to take refuge, as well as people who have actualized the rank of arhat and come to ask about the dharma, will all without fail be given the means to clarify the mind ground. We have not yet heard about this in the various schools. Buddha disciples should just learn buddha-dharma.

Buddha's teaching is not only found in his preaching. As Dōgen Zenji said, "Buddha's disciples should just learn buddha-dharma." Simply sitting zazen as jijuyu zanmai is vital.

How is the situation in the Japanese Sōtō school today? Rinzai monks practice zazen a lot, but Sōtō monks do not practice so much. Priests who experienced zazen a little bit at Komazawa University or who sat for six months or a year at some monastery teach zazen to beginners. This is really ridiculous. "Clear-sighted masters who have attained the way and accord with enlightenment" means teachers who have thoroughly practiced zazen and experienced every nook and cranny of zazen life. A true teacher must really be an out-and-out zazen person.

Even believers or practitioners of other religions come to take refuge in such a person. I myself studied Christianity first, but I couldn't understand the Bible no matter how hard I tried to do so at that time. Later I devotedly practiced zazen with Sawaki Roshi, and after that I realized the meaning of teachings in the Bible. Once I was invited to a Christian school and gave a talk about important points in the Bible. People said my talk was more understandable than a pastor's sermon, and they transcribed it to deliver to Christian believers. Zazen is something like this.

As for "the means to clarify the mind ground," to clarify the mind ground does not mean that during sitting we suddenly feel that the mind eye is opened, we are delighted in ecstasy, and say this is enlightenment.

Recently Professor Heinrich, who is the head of the Philosophy Department at a university in Germany, visited me. In our conversation he brought up the name of a famous scholar. I remembered the person because he had also visited me with a professor from Kyoto University. The person is a philosopher and also a scientist. He is a Nobel Prize recipient.

Professor Heinrich said to me, "That person practiced yoga in India, and he wrote about his experience of levitation. He said his body levitated about three inches off the ground. Can such a thing really happen?"

A world-renowned scholar is like this. I think it will be very difficult for true buddha-dharma to spread widely in this world.

Such a sense as floating in space is nothing other than *makyō* [hallucinations during zazen]. We should understand this when we have such an experience. It is a mistake to observe ourselves and feel as if we are floating, or suddenly get into some fantastic state of psychology. Its only meaning is that we might have such a sensation while we are sitting.

You should also know that we unquestionably lack nothing of unsurpassed bodhi, but although we receive and use it endlessly, because we cannot fully accept it, we mindlessly make our arising views habitual and think of this [buddha-dharma] as an object, thus vainly stumbling on the great way.

This is an important point. We unquestionably lack nothing of unsurpassed bodhi. Being alive like this is itself the life of great nature that lacks nothing. However, because we cannot fully accept it, we are caught up with worldly random business or mundane conventional ideas that set us apart from reality. Consequently we mindlessly make our arising views habitual. We think the secretion from the brain is the owner of ourselves, and we are caught up by illusory thoughts. To think one's body levitates three inches from the floor is really a floating thought. It is no good to think such a state of mind is something desirable in our zazen practice. It is most important in zazen to completely

sit on the ground of life. It is nonsense to say that while sitting, a buddha appeared. Even when various thoughts,
images, or sensations come up, we should awaken to the fact
that there is only a wall in front of our eyes. This is important. This is reality.

We arouse illusory thoughts and grasp buddha-dharma
as an object. We reify abstract concepts and pursue them,
thinking them significant, and finally stumble on reality. We
fall down and mistake our way.

*Because of these views, people see various [illusory] flowers in
the sky, such as believing [buddha's teaching to be only] the twelve-
fold chain of causation of the twenty-five realms of existence, or
never exhausting the doctrines of three vehicles, five vehicles, and
buddha's existence or nonexistence. These views arise endlessly.
You should not think that studying such teachings is the correct
way to practice buddha-dharma.*

Although reality is one, people's ways of viewing things
are divergent. Each one of us has various opinions about
each thing. The twelvefold chain of causation is an explanation of how our life and death, which is full of suffering, has
been caused. The twenty-five realms of existence are
Buddhist categories of realms of samsara in which sentient
beings are transmigrating. The three vehicles are shravaka,
pratyeka buddha, and bodhisattva. The five vehicles are the
above three plus human beings and heavenly beings.
"Buddha's existence or nonexistence" refers to the various
ways to view buddha. Merely to study such Buddhist terminology is not the true way of practicing buddha-dharma.

*On the contrary, when we truly do zazen thoroughly, rely-
ing on the buddha mudra and letting go of all affairs, we transcend the limits of sentimental judgments about delusion and
enlightenment, are not caught up in the [dichotomy of] paths of
ordinary people or sages, and immediately stroll beyond classifications and receive and use great awakening. How can the activities
of those who are involved in the snares of words and phrases compare with this?*

The buddha mudra is zazen in which we actualize the

reality of life. In returning to the reality of life, we relinquish all associations. Since we depart from reality by thinking with our discriminating mind, we let go of our discriminations. Zazen is letting go of thoughts.

However, since we human beings like to be amused by toys, we are apt to think with our brains. When we are not satisfied with our own thought, we read novels written by someone else. Novels are leaders of illusory thoughts. Music is the same.

Since childhood, I have often listened to music on a phonograph. First, the waltz was my favorite music. Next I loved the tango, then symphonies. Finally I thought Gregorian chants were best. After I became a monk I clearly understood that no sound, or zazen, is the highest peak of music.

By the way, I know many music teachers practicing zazen. Many people who have thoroughly pursued some hobby also come to sit. One person fished, gambled, and finally womanized, before he reached the point where just sitting without anything was best, and he began to practice zazen.

Zazen goes beyond discrimination between delusion and enlightenment, ordinary beings and sages. Such dichotomies have meaning only on the basis of convention. In our zazen, we let go of such discrimination. Consequently, we don't try to get rid of delusion or seek after enlightenment. We transcend categorization or discrimination in the relative realm, and receive and use the great bodhi of the reality of life. Do not compare this practice with scholars' theories of religion.

THE DEVELOPMENT OF SCIENCE OR TECHNOLOGY DOES NOT ENABLE HUMANITY TO BE NOBLE

QUESTION FIVE:

Concentration is one of the three basic studies; meditation is one of the six paramitas. Both of these are studied by all bod-

hisattvas from the beginning and practiced regardless of whether they are sharp or dull. So the zazen you now speak of is already included. For what reason do you say the true dharma of the tathagata is consolidated in this [one practice]?

The three basic studies in Buddhism are precepts (*shila*), concentration (samadhi), and wisdom (prajna). The first is to observe buddha's precepts and regulations in the sangha, that is, to refrain from doing anything evil. The second is to settle down in quietness. The third is the wisdom that is brought about by observing precepts and practicing zazen within serenity.

The six paramitas are charity, observing precepts, perseverance, diligence, meditation, and wisdom. A bodhisattva should offer things to others, observe precepts, be patient, be diligent in practice, practice zazen, and endow wisdom for the sake of one's own and others' perfection of the Way.

Thus concentration or meditation, that is zazen, is included in both the three basic studies and the six paramitas. Zazen is only one of the methods all Buddhist practitioners have to learn, isn't it? Why did Dōgen Zenji say zazen is the whole buddha way?

However, Dōgen Zenji's zazen is different from the meditation or concentration in the three basic studies or the six paramitas. How is it different? According to common sense, meditation or concentration is considered to be a means to calm down one's mind, the thoughts—including emotions—produced in our brain. Since thoughts make noise and cause us to worry about one thing or another, we try to calm down. In other words, we try to bring our thoughts under the control of thought itself. This practice takes place on the ground of our thoughts.

However, zazen as buddha-dharma is different. In buddha-dharma we see our brain simply as an organ, the same as the stomach or lungs. An organ is only a tool. It does not work to try to calm down the mind with the mind, no matter how hard we try. It is like trying to pull up a mat on which we are sitting.

We see this when we actually sit. Thoughts well up in our mind ceaselessly like smoke, and the smoke forms images like those on a television. They seem real. We have trouble because we take the illusory pictures to be reality and put ourselves into them. This is like a country theatrical performance. In many dramas, a repulsive villain roughly handles the good person who often plays the principal role. It would be ridiculous if someone in the audience could not stand seeing the plot and jumped onto the stage to beat the villain.

Each of us actually participates in such foolish activities. Thoughts are illusions, and actions are reality, but we are directed to do things by such illusory thoughts. The villain exists on the stage as an illusion, but when we beat the villain that action is reality. Then the drama becomes incoherent and the result is mere confusion.

In our zazen, we don't view our thought on the basis of thought, but put it on the ground of life and see thoughts as mere secretions from our brain. We see the function of secretion as one of the abilities of our life force. We see this by letting go of thought. Therefore, our practice is called silent illumination. In this way our life settles into our life. This is zazen.

In the *Dhammapada* (an early Buddhist text) it says, "The foundation of the self is only the self. There is no foundation outside of the well-regulated self." In Christianity or Islam, the foundation of the self is God. In Buddhism the foundation of the self is only the self. The only thing we have to do is to actualize the true self. In *Genjōkōan*, Dōgen Zenji said the same thing: "To study the buddha way is to study the self." Then what is the true self? That is the reality of the self that is life itself. In zazen, we just sit as life itself and let go of life as it is. This is the well-regulated self.

Having no thoughts is not necessarily good zazen. Thoughts are important as secretions from our brain. Secretion oozes out of life. Secretion is different from excretion of waste matter. In the same way that saliva in the mouth or gastric juice in the stomach is secreted, thoughts oozing out of our brain are an important function of life. But too much secretion of gastric juice causes an ulcer, or even cancer. Excessive secretion of thought is also dangerous for our life. Saliva, gastric juice, and thoughts should ooze in an appropriate amount for a natural condition. That is the most healthy condition for life. Meditation as commonly understood and zazen taught by Dōgen Zenji are different on this point.

"The unsurpassed great dharma of the true dharma eye treasury of the wondrous mind of nirvana" is the buddha-dharma itself. I already spoke about the story of the transmission of the dharma from Shakyamuni to Mahakashyapa. When Shakyamuni picked up a flower and blinked, only Mahakashyapa smiled. The buddha-dharma was transmitted in this way.

Dōgen Zenji said,

You should know that this [zazen] is the complete path of the buddha-dharma, and nothing can compare with it.

Zazen, itself, is the whole way of the buddha-dharma. We should not consider it the same as other practices.

QUESTION SIX:

Among the four different postures, why does Buddhism encourage entering realization through meditation only in sitting?

The four different postures are walking, standing, sitting, and lying down—our day-to-day activities. Why is only sitting important among those four forms?

The other day, a foreigner visited me and said, "I want to practice zazen, but I cannot sit cross-legged. What do you think about sitting on a chair for zazen?" It is not so good. Sitting in full lotus or half lotus position is completely different from sitting on a chair. If you actually sit, you will see the difference. It seems similar, but the mental condition is different. By sitting with crossed legs, the body becomes straightforward, and the mind becomes straightforward too.

In general, because foreigners have longer legs, those who begin to sit in their twenties can sit cross-legged more easily than Japanese. But some people in their thirties seem to have a lot of pain, and there are only a few who can begin sitting in their forties. It is almost impossible for people older than fifty. If people still want to sit, I recommend sitting on a chair as the second-best method. The important point is that they straighten the spine so that they feel as if they place the abdomen on their lap. But this is still different from the real zazen posture. Why do body and mind become straightforward? I cannot explain it with words.

If you seek a reason, you must know that it is only because [sitting] is what has been used by Buddhist practitioners, and beyond this you do not need to search.

I can only say that from ancient times, Buddhist practitioners have valued the zazen posture. I think zazen is a wonderful invention. Nuclear power, jet airplanes, skyscrapers, and many other products of modern civilization do not enable human beings to become noble. People living in modern civilization are doing precisely the same things as primitive people did. How to ennoble humanity is most important. I think zazen is a wonderful invention of the Indian people. Sawaki Roshi said, "When we just do zazen, we emanate a divine atmosphere."

After Sawaki Roshi passed away, I started five-day sesshins in which we only sit. That was in the midst of the hippie generation, and many foreigners came, one by one. At that time, there were few foreigners who spoke Japanese, and we didn't have good translators, so I just taught them the posture of zazen.

An American named Mike Brown came to Antaiji directly from Haneda airport, one day before a sesshin in which we sat fourteen hours a day for five days. I told him that I would allow him to stay if he sat the full sesshin with us. He replied "Yes, I will!" He sat the whole sesshin very enthusiastically, though I thought it was extremely hard for him.

All sorts of foreigners stayed at Antaiji for practice or lived in apartments in the neighborhood and came to sit. They sat without understanding the reason why they had to sit or what zazen really is. Because of the language barrier, I couldn't explain it well for them. Yet they actually sat, I think because they felt something good in zazen.

Some people say that if they practice zazen, their stomach works better or their brain works thirty percent more efficiently. This is evidence that their brains do not work well. What is good in zazen is not such ridiculous effects.

The Ancestor [Nagarjuna] praises it, saying, "Zazen itself is the dharma gate of ease and delight (nirvana)."

We surely have peace in zazen. We have pain in our legs; we are hit if we move; we are forced to sit without rest. Many people may wonder why such a painful practice is the dharma gate of ease and delight. But when we actually sit we somehow feel rather peaceful, more than merely painful. This is why I say zazen is so *yūsui* (profound).

This is not the path of practice of one or two buddhas, but all buddhas and ancestors follow this path.

From beginningless time, innumerable buddhas and all ancestors in the lineage from Shakyamuni have been practicing zazen.

However, in order to continue zazen for one's whole life, it is not enough to feel comfortable. We must thoroughly understand buddha-dharma. Buddha-dharma should be the content of our zazen. We should carefully listen to buddha-dharma in order to practice zazen without deviation.

QUESTION SEVEN:

As for the practice of zazen, people who have not yet realized buddha-dharma should attain enlightenment through practicing the way of zazen. But what could those who have already clarified the true buddha-dharma expect from doing zazen?

This question asks whether or not an already enlightened person still has to practice zazen.

Although it is said that one should not relate dreams to fools and it is useless to give oars to mountain folks, I will give you further instruction.

It's useless to talk to a person who asks such a foolish question. It is pointless to give an oar to a woodcutter. Yet Dōgen Zenji tries to give more instruction. This is his characteristically severe expression, but following it is the most important point.

Thinking that practice and enlightenment are not one is no more than a view that is outside the Way.

"Outside the Way" means non-Buddhist, that is, those who have nothing to do with Buddha's teaching. Such people commonly think that practice is one thing, enlightenment another, and that practice is a means to get enlightenment. People without true understanding of Buddhism think that practice and enlightenment are something like a person wanting to be a barber. First one becomes an apprentice and learns haircutting techniques, and after a certain period of apprenticeship experience, one becomes an independent barber. However, buddha-dharma is not like that.

In buddha-dharma, practice and enlightenment are one and the same. Because it is the practice of enlightenment, a beginner's wholehearted practice of the Way is exactly the totality of original enlightenment. For this reason, in conveying the essential attitude for practice, it is taught not to wait for enlightenment outside practice. This must be so because [this practice] is the directly indicated original enlightenment. Since it is already the enlightenment of practice, enlightenment is endless; since it is the practice of enlightenment, practice is beginningless.

"Directly indicated" sounds peculiar, but it means "that's it" or "as it is." This is exactly original enlightenment, the reality of life.

For example, when I am asked who I am, I may answer that I am Uchiyama Kōshō. But Uchiyama Kōshō is not the reality of myself; it is only my name. I may reply, "I am a Buddhist monk." But being a monk is merely my occupation. It's a strange occupation, isn't it? Anyway, those are not the reality of life, not the directly indicated original enlightenment.

The word *shu* (practice) is often used, but the meaning

is vague. According to a dictionary this word means to put something in order, fix, put things to right, or make things ready. So practice means to fix yourself, put yourself right, and make yourself straightforward. In other words, the reality of life settles down into the reality of life itself. The reality of life becomes straightforward and carries out the reality of life in accordance with the reality of life. In my expression, enlightenment is to **be** the reality of life and practice is to **actualize** the reality of life. Isn't this more understandable?

"In buddha-dharma, practice and enlightenment are one and the same." This sentence means that we actualize the reality of life simply because actualization of the reality of life **is** the reality of life. Since we are living out the reality of life, we actualize the reality of life in accordance with the reality of life. This is practice based on enlightenment (*shushō ichinyo*). Our very first zazen is also the practice of enlightenment. The reality of life is completely manifested within it.

We often think that the beginner's zazen is not good, but with longer practice it will become true zazen. Dōgen Zenji's zazen is not something like that. Even when an inexperienced person sits for the first time, since zazen itself is the posture of the reality of life, that person's zazen is nothing other than actualization of reality. "A beginner's wholehearted practice of the Way is exactly the totality of original enlightenment."

Therefore Dōgen Zenji taught us not to wait for enlightenment outside practice. It is a mistake to think that there is a reality of life outside of the practice of reality. Actualization of reality is only reality. As a matter of course, the practice of zazen itself is the reality of life.

If you practice with the expectation that there is some sort of enlightenment outside of zazen practice, since such an expectation is floating away from reality, your zazen will also part from reality. Letting go of all such expectations, just sit. Just carry out reality. This is our practice.

Sawaki Roshi often talked about practice in this way:

"If you steal something from someone imitating Ishikawa Goemon [a legendary Japanese thief], you directly become a thief." It doesn't work to use the excuse, "I only imitated the action of a thief." At least, such an excuse doesn't work in the realm of religion.

In these days, some politicians do not think that they commit a crime of corruption even when they accept a bribe. Even when they go to the prosecutor's office and are investigated and prosecuted, they think they can hush it up and be cleared of the charge. They are only proud that they have such power, instead of feeling guilty. Even when they are found guilty, they bring a final appeal to the Supreme Court. They try to stall for time as much as possible, and when they are found guilty by the Supreme Court, they finally realize that they are criminals.

However, at least in the religion that is the realm of the reality of life, it is different. As soon as you accept a bribe, you are guilty. In the same way, we don't gradually become a buddha after a long time of practice imitating Shakyamuni. When we sit in zazen, we are immediately buddha. We go directly into buddhahood.

Sawaki Roshi's analogy is easy to understand. It is very interesting to compare Ishikawa Goemon with Shakyamuni.

When I observe Sōtō priests today, I have to add one more point to Sawaki Roshi's comment. To practice zazen imitating Shakyamuni is completely different from showing off the imitation of buddha to people. I don't want to speak ill of Sōtō priests, but there are many of them who show off their zazen. If you have even a slight thought to show off in zazen in front of people, it is not zazen anymore. Chanting nembutsu is the same. There are many priests who begin to chant "Namu Amida Butsu" as soon as some believers come to see them. This is merely business-minded activity.

We often see priests who play the role of priest or religious teacher in front of people. They act as if they are really dignified, faithful, and merciful persons. They perform grand ceremonies and give lofty sermons. Such people are puffed up with pride when their speeches move the audience's heart deeply.

If you speak for the sake of touching an audience's heart, you are simply an actor. The only important thing is to be the self that is only the self. We should carry things out on our own without any associations with others. If we care about others' attention, our practice is no good.

Of course, it is good to sit enthusiastically, but your enthusiasm should not be for competition with others. Then shall we honestly follow our desires? Shall we sit only when we want to sit, and avoid sitting when we don't want to? This is also a mistake. It is good to sit with other people because we have scheduled zazen, even if we don't want to sit on that day. This is worthy zazen. Even if we sit unwillingly or we sit to keep others company, zazen is zazen when we actually sit. It is solely dependent upon your attitude toward practice at the moment. If you sit for the sake of showing off your zazen to others even for an instant, your zazen becomes that of a poor actor.

This is a very subtle point in the realm of religion. Reality is your subtle, inward attitude at the moment. Reality should actualize reality in accordance with reality. You cannot say that whatever you do is reality. In practice, there are mistaken or false realities. So we cannot justify ourselves by saying that whatever we do is reality. First of all, we should always aim at practice in accordance with reality. Aim sincerely for the posture of zazen with your bones and muscles, and let go of thoughts. Only when we have this aim does our zazen become enlivened. Essentially, ever-fresh self returns to ever-fresh self. That's it.

Since a beginner's wholehearted practice of the Way is exactly the totality of original enlightenment, a beginner's first zazen is good enough if one sits in this way. And yet in practice, it is also important to sit for a long period of time.

When I was practicing with Sawaki Roshi, almost every day I thought about whether I should quit being a monk or not. That condition lasted for a long time. Even though I became a monk after I became really determined to devote myself solely to zazen, such thoughts always welled up. But each time, I reconsidered that it was just my thought and I should not be pulled by it.

I suppose that my disciples who are practicing now have the same problems. No matter how many years they stay at Antaiji, they will not get certification as a priest. They get no salary. They cannot expect to get a pension as a matter of course. It is very difficult for young people to stay quietly for even a few years. After seven, eight, or ten years it is very natural for them to have questions about whether to continue practice or not. Furthermore, this kind of question lasts endlessly. Once they start to look for a more interesting way of life, they cannot but pursue other possibilities. Various random ideas arise, one after another, ceaselessly. To let go of such ceaseless thoughts is practice. It is really uneasy practice.

I have been smoking since I was a middle school student. I love smoking. I have tried to quit a number of times. Upon determining to stop smoking, I didn't smoke for several days, then right after I felt I could really stop, I smoked a cigarette. I couldn't quit after all. I muddle on by trying to smoke as little as possible. Zazen practice shouldn't be like this. We cannot quit even for a while, but should continue endlessly though we encounter various situations through which we have to go on practicing.

When I was about forty-two or forty-three years old, there was a woman to whom I was attracted. Since I didn't especially vow to be celibate my whole life, there was no reason why I shouldn't marry her. And yet at the time I had no income at all. I couldn't get married unless I quit practice as a monk and got a job. That was a serious problem for me.

Then I thought that, in many cases, men are attracted by women in the spring. I persuaded myself that this is only a thought of spring, and kept practicing zazen by myself, day after day. The late spring had come; evenings of late spring are teasing even without such a matter. I kept sitting silently in those circumstances. In those days it was completely quiet at Antaiji. A water rail sang in the stillness. I made it through the late spring in this way, and hot summer came and went. When finally autumn had come, I found that my helpless thought had gone before I was aware of it. I said to myself at the time, "That was merely a thought of spring after all."

However, next spring the same thought arose again. I kept sitting and got over it. My mind calmed down again in the fall. I repeated this for three years. I was released from the thought in the fourth year.

Now I think when we are forty-two or forty-three, our physical and mental conditions change, so it is one of the barriers in our lives. I went through it in that manner. It is important to see that our thought for the opposite sex is just a thought of spring secreted by our brain. In order to carry us through, we have to practice zazen and let go of thoughts. We have to actualize reality within reality.

We don't usually live in this way. People fall in love in spring, hold hands within a week, and go further. The result comes in July or August. They have a hectic time thinking about what to do with the baby.

The other day, I received a letter from an old lady. Her husband had been coming to Antaiji to practice since right after I came to Kyoto in 1949. I knew him for more than thirty years. He was really a wonderful person, and he had died recently.

It is not always good to have a nice husband, because this woman's husband was such a gentle person that she became a little bit self-centered. She told me that she was in a hospital and asked me to write her a letter for consolation. I made a call of inquiry on her. She suffered from neuralgia and had terrible pain, especially in the night. Her heart beat so quickly that she felt she might die. At such times she complained by telephone about her pain to her brothers, sisters, or friends, even at midnight.

I told her it was better not to grumble. But it is almost impossible for that kind of person to let go of thought even if told to do so.

I have been physically weak. I often had to spend time in bed. While I was sick, since I couldn't sit I chanted "Namu Kanzeon Bosatsu" as a practice. In the winter of 1945, I stayed in a mountain in Shimane Prefecture and worked producing charcoal. Even when it snowed heavily, I had to go to work in the steep mountains to cut trees and carry them down to the charcoal burner's lodge. I was exhausted from cold, poor nutrition, and hard work. One day when I was in the toilet, I almost unconsciously chanted "Namu Kanzeon Bosatsu." That was the first time I chanted it. After that experience I began to read the Kanzeon Sutra (the twenty-fifth chapter of the Lotus Sutra). Later I wrote a book about this sutra.

The name of the bodhisattva Kanzeon (Avalokiteshvara) is commonly interpreted as "the one who sees (contemplates) the sounds of the world." But I think it is more precise to read it as "the sound that sees (contemplates) the world." The important word here is *kan* (to see, observe, or contemplate), which means to see things without taking any point of view.

In the human world, for example, though every country seeks peace, each country sees a situation from its own one-sided point of view. Consequently people begin to fight, and finally wars arise. Generally speaking, when each side has its own point of view, things that are closer look bigger, and things in the distance look smaller. Eventually each individual opinion does not match the other. *Kan* is not this way of seeing things. We should take out all points of view; true reality will be seen only when all points of view are removed.

"The sound that sees the world" is the sound of chanting "Namu Kanzeon Bosatsu" with our mouth. This is what we practice in zazen, too. For instance, when I chant "Namu Kanzeon Bosatsu," I let go of thought; I relinquish my viewpoint. This is "portable zazen," because I can chant whenever and wherever, even when I have to lie down in bed, walk, or be in the toilet.

"Namu Amida Butsu" is also good. In this case, gratitude for being able to live in all conditions in the whole heaven and earth is emphasized. Chanting nembutsu is the practice of gratitude or repaying indebtedness. Shinran Shōnin said, "I don't know at all whether nembutsu is a practice for going to hell or to the Pure Land." We don't know whether it is beneficial or not for us as individuals, and yet we just chant.

However, is it possible for us to always feel that we are living in the universe of Amitaba Buddha and be grateful for it? I think it is often impossible for us ordinary human beings in our actual day-to-day lives. We are more often apt to think that there is neither buddha nor God in this world, because we have a lot of suffering and miserable experiences.

But those are all my own thoughts. Therefore, we let go of thought and our own viewpoint and chant "Namu Amida Butsu." Then my limited way of viewing things is removed; this is why I say chanting is portable zazen.

When I visit people in bed due to illness, I give them a copy of the sutra of Kanzeon. In the sutra, it is said that when we chant "Namu Kanzeon Bosatsu" we will be released from any kind of suffering. It is also said that if you want to have a good child, chant the name of the bodhisattva and a good baby will be born. Isn't this quite a self-seeking wish?

As a whole, human beings are always self-centered. It is almost impossible to eliminate selfish desires. When we are driven to the last extreme it is only natural to scream for help without thinking. It is absolutely all right to scream for help in such situations, and yet in reality, in most cases, no one will come to help us. Then we may conclude that there is no buddha or God. This conclusion is a mistake.

In the reality of life we scream, "Help me!" Since this is the reality of life, we should be purely as we are. Just screaming is enough. When we suffer, when we have a hard time, or when we are in a desperate situation, we just chant "Namu Kanzeon Bosatsu" in the same way.

I practiced zazen wholeheartedly while I could sit, but when one is aging, it sometimes becomes physically impossible to practice zazen. There are a few wonderful people

like Kato Imashiro who sat a five-day sesshin each month at
Antaiji after he was eighty years old. But generally speaking,
after sixty-five years of age, when most people enter senes-
cence, it becomes hard to sit so much. I suppose that ancient
Indian practitioners practiced zazen when they were young,
and when they became aged and had difficulty sitting they
started to chant nembutsu or *shomyo* (traditional Buddhist
chanting). I don't think chanting and zazen belong to completely separate schools of Buddhism.

> *When I have to struggle seeking*
> * after something,*
> *When I feel loneliness in helpless solitude,*
> *When I am in despair of myself,*
> *—These are all thoughts of ourselves.*
> *Leave everything to zazen, letting go*
> * of thought,*
> *Or to single-minded chanting of the sound*
> * that sees the world.*
> *At this time, even though we don't know it*
> * consciously*
> *Suddenly, whatever has happened*
> *The living reality of the self that is only the self*
> * is there,*
> *Just as the big sky is always the big sky.*

The big sky is always the big sky. Sometimes it is
cloudy; sometimes it rains or snows. But the big sky is
always the big sky. Whatever happens, the sky is just the sky.
This is true gratitude.

We sit in zazen and let go of thought, or we single-
mindedly chant the name of Kanzeon, the sound that sees
the world. At this time, from the viewpoint of our thinking,
we wonder whether we are released or not. We don't know
at all, and yet as we don't know, we are the universal self
that is only the self in whatever situation arises. We remain
determined in this way and keep sitting or chanting. It is all

right if we have doubts about it while practicing. Just keep sitting or chanting.

If we think that we are developing and getting a better state of mind in our zazen, such practice is egotistic zazen. Such a state of mind is, according to Sawaki Roshi, a demon's satori.

On the contrary, buddha is actualized only when ordinary human beings are at a loss. Nonsensical, meaningless, random thoughts always well up in our minds. Even while we wonder whether our zazen is good or bad we can just sit, aiming at not being caught up in such thoughts, because they are just secretions from our brains. Chanting "Namu Kanzeon Bosatsu" is the same.

To speak about chanting is something extra when I talk about *Shōbōgenzō*. But as a practical matter, there are people who cannot physically sit, and I have to tell those people what to do. My talk is not a scholastic lecture on *Shōbōgenzō*.

"Since it is already the enlightenment of practice, enlightenment is endless; since it is the practice of enlightenment, practice is beginningless." Since enlightenment is to settle down in the reality that is actualized in our practice right now, it has no end. Also, as it is practice to actualize reality, there is no beginning.

When we sit we manifest the whole of original enlightenment. It is not a matter of attaining enlightenment gradually as a reward after long practice. Since you and I and all living beings and existences are nothing other than the reality of life, lacking nothing, we just actualize reality. This is zazen practice.

Sawaki Roshi often said, "We don't become better in our zazen. Zazen is to forget good and bad." Almost all people practice zazen in order to become better, but it is not right. Zazen is letting go of thought that discriminates good and bad.

Therefore, both Shakyamuni Tathagata and Venerable Mahakashyapa were accepted and used in the practice of enlight-

*enment, and in the same manner Great Teacher Bodhidharma
and Great Ancestor Daikan [the Sixth Ancestor] were pulled and
turned in the practice of enlightenment. Traces of dwelling in and
maintaining buddha-dharma are all like this.*

"To be pulled and turned" means to go back to the
reality of life and function on its basis.

*Already there is practice not separate from enlightenment,
and fortunately for us, this wholehearted engaging the Way with
beginner's mind, which transmits the undivided wondrous practice, is exactly attaining undivided original enlightenment in the
ground of nonfabrication.*

This is the same thing Dōgen Zenji said in *Genjōkōan:*
"When we attain one dharma, we practice one dharma.
When we encounter one practice, we carry out one practice."
In the *Yuikyōgyō* (The sutra of the last teaching), the Buddha
put emphasis on *pratimoksha* (*betsu gedatsu* in Japanese, or
individual release), which means case-by-case emancipation.
When we observe a certain precept, we are released from the
delusory desire corresponding to that precept. You are
emancipated as much as you practice.

*We must know that, in order not to allow defilement of
enlightenment inseparable from practice, the buddha ancestors
vigilantly teach us not to slacken practice. When wondrous practice
is cast off original enlightenment fills our hands; when we are free
from original enlightenment, wondrous practice is carried out
through the whole body.*

Since enlightenment is in practice, we have to continue
practice ceaselessly and endlessly. But while you are actually
practicing, you shouldn't think that "you" are practicing.
Though you are practicing, you should let go of the thought
of practicing. Within this letting go, the original reality is
actualized; as Dōgen Zenji said, the original enlightenment
fills our hands. Right there, the reality of practice is manifested. This is *shikan* (just doing) practice. From the beginning our self is living out reality. But when we just practice,
letting go of even such an idea and casting off original
enlightenment, then our practice actualizes reality going

beyond reality. At this time, true practice permeates our whole body.

Also, I saw with my own eyes in Great Song China that Zen monasteries in various regions, with from five or six hundred to one or two thousand monks, all had zazen halls and doing zazen day and night was encouraged.

In Song Dynasty China Zen was very popular. There are imposing zazen halls at Zen monasteries in Japan too, though some of them are used as storerooms. I think it is better not to build a zazen hall. Since priests like to play with toys, they often want to build a magnificent zazen hall, but buddha-dharma lies only in practicing the reality of zazen. We can practice the reality of zazen anywhere. Just sitting quietly is enough. In *Zuimonki* Dōgen Zenji also said that construction of imposing buildings has nothing to do with the flourishing of buddha-dharma, but even one or two persons truly practicing zazen is the flourishing of buddha-dharma.

When I asked the teachers transmitting buddha mind mudra and who were in charge of temples about the essence of buddha-dharma, they spoke of the principle that practice and enlightenment are not two.

For this reason I urge not only the practitioners in this tradition but all lofty persons seeking dharma, people wishing for the genuine buddha-dharma regardless of whether they are beginners or advanced, without distinguishing between the ordinary and the sage, to engage in zazen according to the teachings of the buddha ancestors and following the path of masters.

Haven't you heard the ancestral teacher's utterance, "It is not that there is no practice and enlightenment, but only that it cannot be defiled"? Also it was said, "A person who sees the Way practices the Way." You should know that you must practice in the midst of attaining the Way.

We cannot say there is neither practice nor enlightenment, and yet we shouldn't defile the reality; we shouldn't conceptualize the reality. Zazen is zazen only when we actually practice zazen. When we conceptualize it, it becomes stained. At the same time, a person who sees the

Way practices the Way. We can practice the buddha way only when we understand what the buddha way actually is.

Dōgen Zenji again points to something important we "should know." You must practice in the midst of attaining the Way. This means all of us have attained the way as reality, or each of us as we are is living out the reality of life freely without anything lacking. How shall we actualize such reality? How can we manifest the original reality? To work on this matter is our practice.

QUESTION EIGHT:

When all the teachers who spread the teachings in our country in past ages came back from China and introduced Buddhism, why did they put aside this essential practice and only bring back the teachings?

"The teachers . . . in past ages" refers to Japanese priests who went to Tang or Song Dynasty China in the Japanese Nara or Heian periods. They didn't transmit zazen, but only brought back Buddhist philosophy and commentaries on scriptures. Since they went to China after Bodhidharma had come to China, they must have had the chance to encounter Zen practice. Despite that, why didn't they introduce Zen to Japan? Regarding this question, Dōgen Zenji replied that it was because "the time was not yet ripe," and people had not yet matured.

QUESTION NINE:

Did those venerable teachers comprehend this dharma?

A continuation of the last question, this question is about whether those ancient priests truly embodied buddha-dharma or not. Dōgen Zenji replied:

If they had understood, it would have been introduced.

I have to learn this kind of sophisticated expression. If I was in his place, I would have said, "No, those guys didn't understand zazen at all."

QUESTION TEN:

Someone has said, "Do not grieve over life and death. There is an instantaneous means for separating from life and death. It is

175

to understand the principle that mind nature is permanent. This means that even though the body that is born will inevitably be carried into death, still, this mind nature never perishes. If you really understand that the mind nature existing in our body is not subject to birth and death, then since it is the original nature, although the body is only a temporary form haphazardly born here and dying, the mind is permanent and unchangeable in the past, present, and future. To know this is called release from life and death. Those who know this principle will forever extinguish their rounds of life and death, and when their bodies perish they enter into the ocean of original nature. When they stream into this ocean, they are truly endowed with the same wondrous virtues as the buddha-tathagatas. Now even though you know this, because your body was produced by the delusory karma of previous lives, you are not the same as the sages. Those who do not yet know this must forever transmigrate within the realm of life and death. Consequently, you need comprehend only the permanence of mind nature. What can you expect from vainly spending your whole life doing quiet sitting?"

Is such an opinion truly in accord with the Way of buddhas and ancestors?

This is a question about a commonly believed superstition in Dōgen Zenji's time that seems ridiculous to us today. Ancient people must have had so much fear of dying. For them, how to be released from life and death was the matter of primary concern. Consequently, people seriously believed that the body surely dies but mind never dies.

Modern people do not grieve over life and death. People think that to live is to have pleasure. They try to enjoy their lives and never think of death as their own. They only think of others' deaths. They calculate how much money they can inherit when their parents die and anticipate their boss's death, expecting to take his position. But while we neglect our own death and only think of subsistence we can never understand the truth of life; truly we cannot live vigorously.

Shakyamuni questioned life that includes living, aging,

sickness, and death, and began to seek the Way. Only after we awaken to life that includes living, aging, sickness, and dying can we live with true meaning. This is the foundation for thinking about our own life. Yet Shakyamuni's disciples took it for granted that life is miserable only because they were taught that living beings have to die and people we meet have to depart. They interpreted Buddha's teachings as a kind of misanthropic view of life. Shakyamuni must have spoken about the absolute reality of living, aging, sickness, and dying in order to teach others how to live a vigorous life. But since people see death from the ground of desire for existence, dying is only a painful and sad matter. Consequently, such people consider Buddhism pessimistic because it considers life to be living, aging, sickness, and dying. This is a big mistake. Simply because life involves dying, life can be a vivid reality. If we only think of existence and neglect thinking of death, our life is like a plastic flower. It doesn't die, but it has no fragrance, is not animated, and bears no fruit. Gradually it will become filthy and will be thrown away.

The Western way of thinking is entirely based on civilization as existence. Have there been any Western philosophers who thought of their own death? Only existentialists think of death, but they are still newly fledged. Shakyamuni's teaching is much more profound, but today's Japanese do not understand this.

When they are asked why they live, people today often reply that they are seeking happiness. It seems almost everyone is completely devoted to gaining happiness. But to me, happiness as a concept is very childish. Children often say, "I am so happy!" for example when they win a prize in a spelling contest.

First of all, it is a very vague idea so it is difficult to define. A rose-colored feeling of happiness is just a matter of emotion. What will happen to such an emotion when we are dying? When we face death, no one will say, "I am happy." When we die we have to part from status, fame, wealth, family, houses, all of the things we achieved in our whole life. People who have been thinking they spent a happy life have to suffer much more than others. They cannot be happy in front of death. Only other people will say that they were a happy person, that they were so successful and accumulated a lot of wealth and lived long enough.

When we consider the mortality of human beings, it is clear that the concept of happiness is totally useless as a measurement.

The Buddha's true teaching is not pessimism at all. After our own death, happiness and unhappiness, good and bad, hell and paradise, satori and delusion, are all the same. There are no differences among bones. We cannot tell whether a bone was a happy person's or an unhappy person's, or whether the bones belonged to someone beautiful or ugly. There is also no distinction between an enlightened person's bone and a deluded person's bone. There are some people who worship Buddha's relics. That's ridiculous. I have seen Buddha's relics three or four times at different places. There shouldn't be so many of Buddha's relics remaining. I have heard that people produced those relics. In the *Zuimonki*, Dōgen Zenji criticized a monk who worshiped Buddha's relics, saying it was not buddha-dharma but the action of a demon.

The most important point is to put all things, both happiness and unhappiness, enlightenment and delusion, on the same ground. We should think of how we can live on that ground. However, people today pursue happiness and try to escape from unhappiness, seek after enlightenment and try to eliminate delusion. Since they think of life from such a point of view, their life goes off the mark. We should live out the self that is only the self, in whatever situation we face.

I am a more sinful person than others. I don't think I will be able to go to paradise. Also I am always living right within delusion. Am I happy? I cannot say I am happy in the common sense of the word. I earned enough money to pay

income tax only once in my life. That was when I published
a book of *origami* (paper folding) with a big publisher. On
the basis of worldly measurement, financially I am in the
lowest class. Until now I have been living without thinking
of livelihood. When I was young I somehow survived by
crying "Ho!" and being given one yen, five yen, or ten yen
for takuhatsu. Even now I am shuffling along day by day, yet
I look pretty well. It is all right to temporize livelihood and
go through it, but there is one thing you cannot shuffle
along about, that is your attitude toward living the self that
is only the self. It's most important to sit and settle down
with this attitude. To be released from life and death means
having this attitude.

Mind nature has been believed to be eternal and the
soul immortal. Many people thought Buddhism also taught
the same theory, that after death one's soul doesn't die but is
reborn. I suppose all of you understand that Shakyamuni's
teaching was not like that. Transmigration in samsara or
reincarnation was not Shakyamuni's teaching; such a belief
was Indian folk religion from ancient times. True Buddhism
teaches us to be released from transmigration.

In ancient times, people seriously believed that spiritual intelligence or a soul escapes the flesh when a body dies
and enters another creature to be reborn.

I heard the following story from Sawaki Roshi. In the
Tokugawa period the abbot of Sairaiji in Tsu, Mie Prefecture, was once walking, accompanied by a novice. They
came across a couple of dogs copulating. When the abbot
looked at them he shed tears. Since he was the abbot of a big
temple, he must have worn gorgeous robes and okesa, and
his face must have looked merciful. It would be so funny to
see a cartoon with such a priest watching leaping dogs. The
priest seriously said, "Hey, novice, the master of Tabataya
has entered a dog's womb right now." At the time the master of the wealthy merchant family Tabataya in Ise had just
died. When the Tabataya family heard from others that the
priest said the master had entered the dog's womb, they

made a fuss. Later they paid a big sum to buy the puppy born from the female dog, and until its death took good care of it as the incarnation of the master. Of course they made a big donation to the priest.

It may sound like a fairy tale to today's people, but this kind of story still exists in America, which is one of the most developed countries. Sometimes someone relates such stories to me. It is interesting that they use computers or videotapes as evidence in order to make people believe such stories.

Sawaki Roshi said, "Someone asked me whether ghosts exist in the world or not. People who ask such a question are ghosts." I agree with Sawaki Roshi.

The admonition of Nanyang Huizhong (d. 775, Chinese National Teacher, Nanyō Echū in Japanese) is discussed by Dōgen Zenji in *Shōbōgenzō Sokushin Zebutsu* (Mind itself is buddha). In short, the reality of life cannot be separated into dichotomies such as mind and body, happiness and unhappiness, hell and paradise, enlightenment and delusion. Such discrimination is caused by our brain.

Usually we try to handle the reality of life with our brain. However, since the reality of life includes the mind, it is impossible to deal with the reality of life with the brain. Consequently, we should think how to live in the ground that includes both hell and paradise, enlightenment and delusion, life and death. On that basis we can live vigorously. It's no good to live with desires to depart delusions, with fear of hell, or with the wish to escape from death.

Even today, the kinds of non-Buddhist religions that teach that the mind is eternal but the body mortal are popular. Among Buddhist believers or even priests who are considered Buddha's disciples, there are some who do not understand the difference between Buddhism and such religions. Such priests should quit being Buddhist.

You should know that fundamentally in buddha-dharma it is affirmed that body and mind are one, essence and material form are not two, and you should have no doubt whatsoever that this is similarly understood in India and in China.

This is the foundation of Buddha's teachings. Reality is never two but one.

Moreover, in the gate of speaking of permanence, all the ten thousand dharmas are permanent, body and mind are not separate. In the gate of speaking about impermanence all dharmas are impermanent, essence and material form are not separate.

Therefore, when we see eternity, everything is eternal. When we see impermanence, everything is impermanent. In other words, the reality of life has no birth, no extension, and yet it is coming and going (tathagata). Though coming and going, it has no going and no coming. In the *Hannya Shingyō* (Heart sutra) we read, "No birth, no extinction, no increasing, no decreasing." Whatever situation we are in, the self that is only the self has no going, no coming. Then doesn't it move? Yes, it is going and coming. It's always moving.

Not only that, you should completely awaken to life and death as exactly nirvana.

In buddha-dharma, life and death is nothing other than nirvana. Life and death and nirvana are not separate things. But people today only see existence and avoid facing death. We cannot talk about true life while we are living with such an attitude.

"The dharma gate of the vast total aspect of mind essence" is a quotation from the *Daijō Kishin Ron* (Awakening of faith of Mahayana). It says in the text, "Mind as suchness is nothing other than the essence of the dharma gate of the vast total aspect." This means that there is nothing but my life in the universe.

It includes the whole vast dharma realm without separating essence and appearance and without speaking of arising and ceasing. [From life and death] up to and including bodhi and nirvana, there is nothing that is not mind essence.

"The whole vast dharma realm" means everything, the whole of life itself. This is the same as the wondrous dharma we saw in the beginning of *Bendōwa*. Since dharma includes everything, we cannot separate essence from appearance, living from death. Everything in its entirety is mind nature.

Without exception, all the myriad phenomena in the entire universe are nothing other than this one mind, with everything included and interconnected.

I always translate this one mind as life, but this life is neither physiological life nor psychological life. Since one mind is all dharmas, and all dharmas are one mind, we should call it simply life.

These various dharma gateways are all equally this one mind. Saying there is no difference at all [between essence and appearance] is exactly how Buddhists understand mind essence.

In Buddhism, mind nature (essence) is never understood as psychological mind. Mind nature is undivided life as a whole, the whole world in which we are living.

BUDDHISM SHOULD START FROM SEEKING THE TRUTH OF ONE'S OWN LIFE

QUESTION ELEVEN:
Is it necessary for those who focus on this zazen to observe the precepts strictly?

REPLY:
The sacred practice of maintaining the precepts is indeed the guiding rule of the Zen gate and the traditional style of buddhas and ancestors, but even those who have not yet received precepts or who have broken the precepts still do not lack the possibility [to practice zazen].

In this question the meaning of precepts is discussed. Maintaining precepts is standard in the tradition of Zen monks and the lifestyle of buddhas and ancestors. Therefore, as a matter of course, zazen practitioners should spend everyday life observing precepts. Yet this doesn't mean people who haven't yet received precepts or people who violate precepts should not practice zazen.

Precepts (*kai* in Japanese, *shila* in Sanskrit) and regulations (*ritsu* in Japanese, *vinaya* in Sanskrit) are a little bit different from each other. Precepts are for refraining from doing evil things; regulations are rules for the community life of monks and nuns.

When many people became Shakyamuni's disciples and formed a sangha, regulations—such as having a meal only once a day before noon, or wearing an okesa—were established. Some of those were probably determined by Shakyamuni himself, but many details were gradually established by disciples in later generations. In the *vinaya* of early Buddhist schools before the Mahayana, there were 248 precepts and regulations for male monks. One of them is that monks should not touch any money. In Theravada tradition, I believe monks still don't have money with them.

Such precepts and regulations were first established in India at the time of Shakyamuni and were later transmitted to China and Japan. The passing of time and differences in the climate and cultural background of each country necessitated changes; some regulations were made in China or Japan.

The fundamental spirit of the precept in Chinese and Japanese Zen originated with Bodhidharma's one mind precepts. In the beginning of the *Isshin Kaimon* (Comments on one mind precepts) it says, "To receive [the precepts] is to transmit [the precepts]. To transmit [the precepts] is to awaken [to the buddha mind]. Therefore, to receive the precepts in their true sense is to realize buddha mind." This is the most essential point. Observing precepts is not simply a matter of social morality or something we should do or shouldn't do.

The ten one mind precepts are as follows.

1. Self nature is wondrous and imperceptible. Within the everlasting dharma, not arousing the view of extinction is called the precept of not killing.

Self nature is what I call the reality of life. Since the

reality of life cannot be grasped by words, it is said to be wondrous and imperceptible. Within this world, in whatever situation, everything is the reality of life. The reality of life cannot be killed by any means. The precept of not killing means that since all beings are in the reality of life, we cannot kill anything. When you don't awaken to the reality and kill some creature, it is a violation of this precept.

> 2. Self nature is wondrous and imperceptible. Within the ungraspable dharma, not arousing the thought of gaining is called the precept of not stealing.

There is nothing we can truly possess as our own. Not thinking "such and such is my property" is to uphold the precept of not stealing.

> 3. Self nature is wondrous and imperceptible. Within the dharma that is free from attachment, not arousing a desire to attach oneself to anyone is called the precept of not having sexual desire.

No man or woman can be, in reality, a possession of someone else as lover or wife or husband. Not holding onto sexual desire is not having such attachment.

> 4. Self nature is wondrous and imperceptible. Within the inexplicable dharma, not speaking a single word is called the precept of not speaking falsehood.

In every situation, everything is nothing other than the reality of life. We cannot explain reality with words. Despite that, to say it is this or that with a one-sided point of view is called speaking falsehoods.

> 5. Self nature is wondrous and imperceptible. Within the intrinsically pure dharma, not being blinded by ignorance is called the precept of not drinking intoxicating liquor.

All things are completely pure and never stained, and yet we defile them with our ignorance. In Mahayana

Buddhism, this precept is called the precept of not selling liquor. This does not simply mean we should not sell alcohol, but it means we should not spread thoughts or ideas that make people drunk or blind.

> 6. Self nature is wondrous and imperceptible. Within the flawless dharma, not speaking of others' faults is called the precept of not speaking of the faults of the four kinds of members [of a sangha].

The reality of life never makes a mistake or sins. Therefore, we don't speak of mistakes or sinning.

> 7. Self nature is wondrous and imperceptible. Within the nondiscriminating dharma, not distinguishing oneself from others is called the precept of not praising oneself nor slandering others.

Everything is equal as the reality of life. If we discriminate ourselves from others, we violate this precept.

> 8. Self nature is wondrous and imperceptible. Within the dharma that is the all-pervading true reality, not arousing greed is called the precept of not begrudging [dharma or material].

We don't attach ourselves to things and begrudge them to others because the reality of life permeates the whole universe.

> 9. Self nature is wondrous and imperceptible. Within the egoless dharma, not substantializing the ego is called the precept of not being angry.

Since everything is the reality of life, there is no "I." Although this precept is commonly understood as not becoming angry, it really means that there is no ego that becomes angry.

> 10. Self nature is wondrous and imperceptible. Within the

dharma that is the single reality, not arousing a dualistic view
of sentient beings and buddhas is called the precept of not
slandering the Three Treasures.

Not slandering the Three Treasures (buddha, dharma,
and sangha) is not discriminating buddha from ordinary sentient beings, which equally abide within the realm of the one
reality.

These are Bodhidharma's one mind precepts. The fundamental attitude of "self nature is wondrous and imperceptible" is most important here. That is, we must see the life of
the self thoroughly and settle on the ground of the reality of
life. This is zazen, and zazen is the foundation for all precepts.

Since I always talk about the reality of life in this manner, people sometimes criticize me, saying, "You don't talk
about what we should do or shouldn't do in a concrete,
moralistic way. We want to listen to good sermons like
that." It does seem that people would like to hear such
"good" sermons. Today's popular religions for this mass
society never talk about reality beyond social morals. They
always tell "good" stories. People like to hear about how
they can become better, and they are not satisfied unless
they gain something better for themselves. However, if we
talk about how we as individuals can become better, it is
only a matter of individual self; it has nothing to do with
buddha-dharma.

Sawaki Roshi said, "It is no good that ordinary people
become enlightened because ordinary people get divine
power." Buddha-dharma never makes ordinary people
greater. Anyway this "I" is an ordinary, deluded human
being. And yet this ordinary person is not separate from
Shakyamuni Buddha. This ordinary person sits on the
ground that is beyond the dichotomy of buddha and ordinary beings. This is buddha-dharma.

I repeat this many times because it is so important.
Although many people think that to practice buddha-
dharma is to eliminate delusions and attain enlightenment,

Dōgen Zenji's buddha-dharma is beyond the dichotomy of delusion and enlightenment. In our zazen, we immovably settle far from such discriminations.

Consequently, precepts as buddha-dharma are not a collection of items about "should" and "should not," but express our fundamental attitude toward life. This is the meaning of "Zen and precepts are one" (*zenkai ichinyo*). We do not judge whether or not a person is qualified to practice zazen on the basis of whether the person has received and observed the precepts or violated them. Even those who have violated precepts before or have not yet received precepts are observing the precepts when they sit in zazen.

QUESTION TWELVE:

Will it be a problem if people who work diligently at this zazen also combine it with practicing Shingon or shikan?

Isn't it better to practice zazen combined with Shingon (mantra) or *shikan* (*shamatha* and *vipashyana* in Sanskrit) rather than simply practicing zazen? Why isn't it good to practice zazen along with nembutsu?

There are some people in this world who try to do everything good. Someone who has a dōjō to practice various good things sends me the dōjō's newsletter each month. They practice zazen, of course, and Okada method breathing, brown rice diet, vegetarian diet, acupuncture, and moxa, in addition to listening to beautiful music, because even cows give milk well when they hear music. This is miscellaneous practice. Shinran Shōnin, the founder of the Jōdō Shin sect, was great because he cast away all miscellaneous practice and concentrated only on faith in Amitabha.

During World War II, I went back to my parents because I suffered from malnutrition. When I recovered a little bit, we decided to make pounded rice cake. Since they had evacuated us from Tokyo to the countryside for safety, we didn't have the proper equipment. But my father was a very industrious person. He began to make a steaming basket. There is usually only one hole at the bottom of such a steaming basket. When I saw him making a hole I said, "It must be more efficient to have more holes." My father agreed with my opinion and made many holes. After he completed it, he put the steaming basket on a pot filled with boiling water and made a fire. The rice never became steamed. From this experience I learned that there should be only one hole in a steaming basket. People knew from the wisdom of experience since ancient times that steam goes through one hole and the inside of a steaming basket becomes hot.

Truly, if you do not engage in one thing, you will never reach one wisdom.

This is very true. In Shingon practice, there is a *dharani* (a long mantra or powerful incantation) with the name *Hajigokumon dharani* (*dharani* for breaking the gate of hell). It is said that when one chants the dharani even the gate of hell will be broken, and one will be able to escape hell. My way of expressing it is, "If we go to hell we should make our mind settle down right there and work through it. Once we have such a decisive attitude, the gate of hell will be broken." In short, it is important to concentrate on one practice.

If we practice zazen, we should practice only zazen. If we practice nembutsu we should completely devote ourselves to chanting nembutsu. If we practice dharani, we should wholeheartedly chant them. In Buddhism we choose one practice and concentrate on it.

QUESTION THIRTEEN:

Can this practice be carried out also by male and female laypeople, or can it only be practiced by monks?

This question is about whether zazen is practice for only monks, or whether laypeople can also practice it. Japanese people have a preconception that Buddhism is something special for a special kind of person. I repeat that the starting point of Buddhism is searching after the truth of the life of one's self. Since it is the truth of the life of each self, it is only natural not to distinguish old from young, men from women, or noble birth from humble birth. Buddhism lies behind our practice of zazen. Behind Buddhism, there should be one's own life. It is essential to see Buddhism from the ground of our own lives and to examine our zazen on the basis of Buddhism. In doing so, it is very apparent that the idea that we can attain some special satori like a superhuman power is off the mark.

Buddhism should not discriminate between men and women, or between upper-class and lower-class people. It is a mistake to consider rich people better than poor people. So we can see it is no good to call for a lot of money in order to practice. This is why I say we shouldn't build special zazen halls. On the basis of the life of the ever-fresh self, it is all right to sit in a field without wearing any special robe. Shakyamuni said a monk's robe is good enough if it covers the body between the breast and knees. Monks didn't need to worry about robes being stolen, since their robes were made out of abandoned rags.

These days many priests' okesas are like luxurious art works, and are very expensive. Priests easily attach themselves to their robes. Even something like this makes priests go in a mistaken direction.

It is the same with a zazen hall. You may think it is good to build one since Japan is a rich country now. It would not matter so much if priests paid for the construction, but they build a zazen hall with money they have collected from laypeople. From the laypeople's point of view, they have to be careful when they go to a temple or they will be taken for their money. In this case, laypeople cannot visit temples without fear. These days there are too many cases of priests alienating laypeople from the temple because of their greed. If so, it is impossible to enlarge the circle of zazen members at a temple.

If we want to propagate zazen, the priest himself has to sit sincerely. In my case, Antaiji was a penniless temple. While Sawaki Roshi was alive he paid for repairing the temple buildings if it was needed. But after Roshi died I couldn't expect anyone to support me in taking care of the temple buildings. Then I made up my mind never to ask for donations from laypeople even if I couldn't repair the temple buildings and they fell apart. I would rather die a heroic death in the battle of zazen. In order to do that, I had to practice zazen as much as possible.

From the outset, since zazen produces nothing, we shouldn't ask people to make a donation. Because of this, I started five-day sesshins with a policy that we didn't charge participants even though we served meals. I named the sesshin *sannai sesshin* (inside the temple sesshin) because I decided to sit the sesshin only with monks staying at Antaiji. We had fewer than ten monks. Once this started, about thirty people came unexpectedly to sit with us from outside. Later the number of people gradually increased to seventy or eighty. Sometimes we had ninety people.

Then, without asking, someone offered the money for expenses for the sesshin when he learned so many people came to sit. Another made a donation in order to extend the main hall and the dormitory. Finally, instead of dying in battle, I enlarged the temple buildings. I will never forget the favor of those people. I want to leave a note of the donors' names before my death, and yet I haven't done it because the time is not yet ripe.

Anyway, what I want to say is that we shouldn't make zazen something special, such as only being able to do zazen inside of a formal zazen hall. We should think of zazen on the ground of the life of each of our selves. We should examine buddha-dharma on the basis of our own life, and examine zazen on the basis of the buddha-dharma.

AFTER ALL, THE BUDDHA WAY IS JUST LIVING OUT THE ORDINARY REALITY OF LIFE

QUESTION FOURTEEN:
Monks quickly depart from their involvements and have no obstacles to wholeheartedly engaging in the way of zazen. But how

can people who are busy with their duties in the world single-mindedly practice and be in accord with the buddha way of nonaction?

If you were a monk who left the mundane world, you would be able to practice easily without the nuisance of worldly duties. But how is it possible for laypeople, always busy with worldly business, to practice?

Here I have to talk about the buddha way of nonaction. The buddha way is, after all, the reality of life. Therefore we should just live out that life as nothing special, the very ordinary reality of life. People lose sight of the fact that it is best to be ordinary. They think something with a special color is better than something plain.

However, it is good for your stomach when you forget the existence of the stomach and let it function well. Also, suppose that you have a small injury on the tip of your little finger. The finger you usually forget will suddenly become a big problem. The best condition for all parts of the body is that you forget the existence of the body and let each part function in accordance with necessity in each situation. This is called nonaction. Just the ordinary reality of life that has nothing special is best.

Yet it is difficult to be exactly as life is. We think of this or that with our brain, though what we think is not reality. Suppose that we now have two hundred yen. If we think about how to get more money, or if we have an inferiority complex because of poverty, we are apart from reality. The reality is the fact that we have two hundred yen.

Then is thinking bad? No, it definitely isn't bad! The true reality of human life is that we are living with a brain. What we think in our brain is not reality but illusion. However, the fact that we have a brain and that the brain functions and produces thoughts is reality. This point gives us the most difficulty when we try to live in accordance with the reality of human life. Knowing that what we think is illusion, we must allow our brain to keep vividly working because this is the reality of life without human fabrication.

Certainly, the buddha ancestors with their great sympathy keep open the vast gate of compassion in order to allow all living beings to enter enlightenment. So which of the various beings would not enter?

The vast gate of compassion is our zazen. It is off the mark to practice zazen in order to scrape away thoughts and enter the stage of no-mind and no-thought. If you really want to be mindless or thoughtless, I'll recommend a very easy method to you. Have an operation to remove your brain and become a vegetable.

Our zazen is different. We keep our brain functioning vividly as it is, and yet we are not caught up in the illusory thoughts. This is the posture of zazen, of letting go of thought. Even though we let go of thought, of course thoughts well up ceaselessly, and yet we don't put ourselves into them. We just keep actualizing the reality of life.

For example, when you drive a car you don't think of what to do moment by moment. You let go of thought, don't you? If you eliminate your thoughts, you fall asleep. If you are caught up in particular thoughts, you will be tense. Both are dangerous. You first of all have to learn the basic techniques for driving a car. You should let your brain work to its full capacity, using your hands and feet to master how to handle the steering wheel, accelerator pedal, brake pedal, and shifting gears. After that, you go out to drive in the town. The scenery in the town changes moment by moment. Pedestrians walk in different directions, and you come across cars going in the opposite direction. Some cars may merge in from side streets, roads may become wider or narrower, and you have to make left or right turns. In each situation, which changes moment by moment, your brain must work vividly, and yet your hands and feet have to move almost automatically without thinking what to do for each action.

I heard from a person who learned to drive in America that his driving teacher said that harmony is most important in order not to disturb others.

I cannot drive a car, but I think driving a car safely is wonderful as a practice. We have to try to live our lives in the same way. The foundation for this is zazen.

If we search, there are many examples of this from antiquity to the present. For instance, although the Emperors Daiso and Junso were fully occupied with many functions during their reigns, they diligently practiced zazen and were proficient in the great way of the buddha ancestors. Also Prime Ministers Ri and Bo, although they served in positions as imperial aides and were highly trusted retainers of emperors, diligently practiced zazen and entered the enlightenment of the great way of buddha ancestors. This only depends on whether or not one has aspiration, without relationship to being a monk or layperson.

The important point in this paragraph is that it depends only on whether or not one has aspiration. As a weak person, I feel small when I hear this kind of statement. When I was about twenty-eight or twenty-nine, I thoroughly reflected on myself and came to know that I am a feeble-minded, useless, and completely good-for-nothing person. At the time, I read *Shōbōgenzō Keiteki*, a commentary on the *Shōbōgenzō* by Zen Master Nishiari Bokusan (1821–1910), and *Emile* by Jean-Jacques Rousseau (the French political philosopher and writer, 1712–1778). Those books influenced me to make up my mind to become a monk.

Keiteki and *Emile* are a unique combination, aren't they? Since my childhood, I had been overprotected, much the same way as Japanese children are today. I only knew how to criticize or blame other people's faults, and yet I couldn't do anything by myself. When I read *Emile*, I understood that such a way of raising children makes them separate from nature. Rousseau insisted on going back to nature. It seems there were many such overprotected children in upper-class families in eighteenth-century France. When they played outside they were always watched by their mothers or maids and warned "It's dangerous!" or "Don't go there!" Consequently, they never had real experiences of danger and only understood the concept of danger from their protectors' words. Eventually they grew up without having the experience of encountering dangerous situations and getting out of such situations by their own efforts. This is what I mean when I say "separate from nature."

Because I grew up in a similar way, I still have no capacity for athletics; I cannot even ride a bicycle. When I throw a ball, no one can tell in which direction it will fly. Whatever I try to do throws me into confusion. When I was about thirty years old, I first understood that it was impossible to live under such conditions. I wanted to go back to nature by any means. I read *Keiteki* at the same time and made up my mind to put myself into the practice life of a monk.

In a monastery, no matter how weak our determination may be, we have to get up at four o'clock in the morning when we hear the wake-up bell. No matter how tired we may be, we have to go to the zazen hall to sit. Even in July or August during the hottest time of the year, we have to wear various robes, Japanese *kimono*, Chinese *koromo*, and Indian *okesa*, and sit in zazen. Since all monks in the assembly do the same things in the same way, we have to always work together in harmony with others even if we don't like the work or the people. Somehow we can do it. This is the so-called divine power of the assembly.

Because I was a good-for-nothing person, I never had the praiseworthy resolution to lead monks in doing things. When I was ordained, I only decided to try to follow other monks in some way.

Unexpectedly, the day I was ordained as a monk was December 8, 1941; that is, Pearl Harbor Day. The war took place. Senior monks were drafted and went into the army or were requisitioned to work for the government, so that they left the monastery. Only the useless monks like me remained. When Japan was losing the war, the circumstances became worse and worse. Especially right after Japan lost the war, we were in the worst condition. No matter how resolved one might be, practitioners couldn't overcome such difficulties only with Way-seeking mind or willpower. All monks began to do different things according to their preference. Though I expected to be led by the divine power of assembly, I couldn't rely on the other monks anymore. Moreover, I found that I would lose direction if I did things with them. Then I reconsidered. After all, I could rely only on myself. No one could live my life for me. Furthermore, I hadn't solved the problem of death. If I couldn't rely on the community of practitioners, I would have to face my own death by myself. If I stopped practice halfway, I would have terrible fear when I had to die.

That was the final impetus. After all, practice should be done by oneself. Only I can live my own life and die my own death. I couldn't help but continue to practice. It was not a matter of whether I have strong willpower or not. The important point is to do it right now. Then the world completely changes. Zazen is mysterious. As Dōgen Zenji said in *Shōbōgenzō Zanmai Ō Zanmai*, "We must know that the whole world of zazen and the whole world of other things are totally different. Realizing this, we must clarify and affirm the arousing of the bodhi mind, practice, awareness, and nirvana of the buddhas and ancestors." The world of zazen and the world of other things are entirely different. Ordinary beings' resolutions don't work. Practicing zazen is, itself, arousing bodhi mind or Way-seeking mind. It's no good to try to practice and attain enlightenment by "my" power. It must be just the practice of zazen and the enlightenment of zazen. Within the world of zazen, everything is zazen.

When we sit, the world of zazen is opened as much as we sit. Therefore, it has nothing to do with whether we are weak-minded or strong-minded. Numbers of people became my disciples, probably only because I guarantee that the world of zazen opens even when a weak person like me practices zazen. My disciples must think they are stronger than I. Therefore they can become my disciples without worrying about whether they can be a real Zen monk or not. Now I think my experience can be a good example for them in terms of encouraging them. This is what is meant by "this only depends on whether or not one has aspiration."

The world of zazen is gracious. In Pure Land Buddhism, when we chant "Namu Amida Butsu" we are pulled along by the power of Amitabha Buddha. In the same way, when we just sit we are pulled along by the power of zazen. This is the whole world of zazen.

Also, anyone who can deeply discern what is important or trivial will thereby have this faith. Needless to say, people who think secular duties interfere with buddha-dharma only know that there is no buddha-dharma in the secular realm, and do not yet realize that there is nothing secular in the realm of buddha.

I remember a person whose name was Ono Shinji when I read this part. He visited Antaiji in 1951 or 1952. After he retired from the National Railway at the required age limit, he began to work for a printing company in Osaka. So he was in his sixties. His work at the company was very different from what he had done at the National Railway. For the sake of the company, he had to become a liar. When he was asked to complete something by a certain date, he had to take the order even though he knew it was impossible. On the appointed day, he had to tell a false story as an excuse. When he made payments, he also had to give false reasons and try to beat down the amount of money even a little. I suppose that small companies that have severe competition with rivals are more or less like this.

When he entered such a business world, he was seriously afflicted. At the time, he heard that there was a dōjō of Sawaki Roshi's in Kyoto, and he visited Antaiji around August. As Sawaki Roshi was absent, I talked with him about his trouble. I said to him, "In *Bendōwa*, Dōgen Zenji said that there is no buddha-dharma in the secular world, and yet there is nothing secular in the world of buddha-dharma. Why don't you practice zazen so as to enter the world of buddha-dharma in which there is nothing mundane?"

He sat with me right after the conversation and began

to sob while sitting. I thought he might go out of his mind, but he didn't. He was thoroughly convinced by what I said, and settled down in the world of buddha-dharma. After that, he practiced zazen without any doubt while he continued to work for the company. When I had sesshin, he took days off and sat with me for three days every month. I always sat sesshins only with him and another student. He continued to come for practice enthusiastically, and often said to the visiting laypeople that there is no buddha-dharma in the secular world, and yet there is nothing secular in the world of buddha-dharma.

Later I found that numbers of older people were deeply moved by this phrase. Human beings do not get older meaninglessly. Of course, not all aged people get old with meaning. There are some deeply deluded people in their seventies or eighties, but certainly there are some who completely understand this.

Young people cannot understand this so easily. They have to practice hard for ten or twenty years. Since they have the many and various problems of youth, they cannot be convinced by such a simple phrase.

If there are some good points in my talk that are understandable to young people, I think that is because my practice started as a result of troubles I had in my own youth. This is the reason I tell my disciples to sit silently for twenty or thirty years.

Laypeople's practice is all right as it is; that is, to sit as much as they have time. But monks have a responsibility to become locomotives that pull people. So they must have strong power, and they must not deviate in practice. It is not permissible for monks to lose their direction while they are leading others. But with the exception of becoming such locomotives, laypeople can practice Dōgen Zenji's zazen just as monks can.

I wonder how many times I thought a weak-willed person like myself was no good. I still think so, but that is gratuitous when we sit and our world becomes the world of zazen. In zazen we have to let go of thoughts that are our own measurements or value judgements, saying, "I am no good," or "I despair of myself."

Recently in China there was a minister of state named Hou, a high official who was experienced in the Ancestral Way. He wrote a poem expressing himself:

> In my spare time from state affairs I enjoy zazen,
>> and hardly sleep lying down on the bed.
> Although still manifesting the appearance of a government official,
> My name has pervaded the four oceans as a senior adept.

Although this person had no rest from his official duties, because of his deep aspiration he attained the buddha way. Seeing others, examine yourself; reflect the ancient in the present.

In Great Song China nowadays, the Emperor and great ministers, educated and common people, men and women, all are attentive to the Ancestral Way. Military and civilian officials all aspire to study the Way in Zen practice. Of those who so aspire, many will certainly open and clarify the mind ground. Obviously this shows that secular duties do not obstruct buddha-dharma.

Dōgen Zenji picked up some examples of lay practitioners who clarified the mind ground because of their aspiration, although they were busy with their duties. At the time in Song China, Zen was very popular; it seems many of the military and civilian officers aspired to practice the way of zazen.

Clarifying the mind ground is not some sort of psychological change through some sudden experience. It means that the world of zazen opens when we let go of our value judgments. Furthermore, by letting go of thought, our attitude toward life will change, and we will begin to live out the reality of life. This is clarifying the mind ground.

If the genuine buddha-dharma permeates the country, because of the ceaseless protection of buddhas and heavenly beings, the emperor's reign will be peaceful.

I agree, and yet if we try to spread buddha-dharma in order to pacify the world, the order will be turned upside down. That is what so-called new religions do in order to collect people. When zazen practice permeates the world, meaningless conflicts may disappear. Consequently, peace may pervade the world. It may be possible, but such an effect is nothing other than a by-product of zazen. We should not put the cart before the horse.

These days, some companies force employees to practice zazen at Zen temples for the sake of making them obedient, so that they work more efficiently without going on strike. Such zazen has nothing to do with buddha-dharma. Zazen should be strictly good for nothing. It is vital to just practice this good-for-nothing practice.

If the reign is peaceful, buddha-dharma attains its strength.

When many laypeople practice zazen and study the buddha way, the buddha-dharma really flourishes.

There are four categories in which to consider monks and laypeople. The first is laypeople with lay mind. They live without any interest in buddha-dharma. The second is monks with monks' mind. They are the powerful locomotives who are leaders of all human beings on the earth. The third is monks with lay mind. They are monks only in appearance and in their job. They are not interested in buddha-dharma at all and are no different from laypeople who seek after fame and profit. When the number of such monks increases, buddha-dharma declines. The fourth is laypeople with monks' mind. They are laypeople, but they have a monk's heart and devote themselves to zazen. When there are many such laypeople, the buddha-dharma certainly flourishes. I hope the number of such bodhisattvas goes on increasing.

Also, during Shakyamuni's stay in the world, even the worst criminals and those with harmful views gained the Way. In the assemblies of ancestral teachers, even hunters and woodcutters realized satori. Needless to say, other people can do this. Just seek the guidance of a true teacher.

The "worst criminal" here refers to King Ajatasatru, who was corrupted by Devadatta and killed his own father,

King Bimbisara. But King Ajatasatru later became one of Shakyamuni's students.

"Those with harmful views" refers to people like Angulimala. When he was a brahman, he was tempted by his teacher's wife, but he rejected her. The wife told tales to her husband and said, "He tried to violate me." In anger, his teacher said to Angulimala, "If you kill a thousand people and make a necklace with their fingers, you will become a sage." Angulimala believed his teacher and killed nine hundred and ninety-nine people. When he was about to kill the thousandth, his own mother, he was persuaded to desist by Shakyamuni. He awoke to his fault and became Shakyamuni's disciple.

An example of a hunter is Sekkyō Ezō (Shigong Huican in Chinese), who was a disciple of Baso Doitsu (Mazu Daoyi). The woodcutter refers to the Sixth Ancestor.

Even such humble people attained the Way. We can understand from these examples that receiving instruction from a true teacher is essential.

LIVING OUT THIS SELF THAT IS UNIVERSAL AND AT THE SAME TIME IS THE POINT OF NOTHINGNESS

QUESTION FIFTEEN:

Even in this corrupt declining age of the world, is it possible to attain enlightenment through this practice?

REPLY:

In the Teaching Schools they focus on various classification systems, yet in the true teaching of Mahayana there is no distinction of True, Semblance, and Final Dharma, and it is said that all who practice will attain the Way.

In this question the expression "this corrupt declining age" is discussed. In one doctrine of Buddhism, the history of Buddhism is divided into three periods. The first five hundred years after Shakyamuni's death is called True Dharma (*shōbō*), the second five hundred or thousand years is called Semblance Dharma (*zōbō*), and the last period is called the Last Dharma (*mappō*). In the age of True Dharma buddha-dharma is correctly practiced. In the age of Semblance Dharma people only practice as a form, and no one attains enlightenment. In the age of the Last Dharma no one practices, only teachings as scriptures remain. People in Dōgen Zenji's time thought they were in the age of the Last Dharma.

These are merely categories created by Buddhist scholars. When we see buddha-dharma on the ground of the life of the self, it is total nonsense to make such distinctions and say that we cannot attain enlightenment no matter how hard we practice. Buddha-dharma is not an outward or social matter; it is the matter of one's self. In whatever age, all who practice will attain the Way.

Especially in this simply transmitted true dharma, both in entering dharma and in embodying it freely, we receive and use our own family treasure.

Zazen is simply jijuyu zanmai, which is life living the reality of life. All is inside ourselves. So whether we attain enlightenment or not is known only to ourselves. As it is said:

Only those who practice know on their own whether they attain enlightenment or not, just as those who use water notice on their own if it is cold or warm.

It is simply like knowing whether water is cold or warm when we actually put our hand in the water. There is no special enlightenment; our actual zazen is enlightenment itself.

QUESTION SIXTEEN:

Someone said, "In buddha-dharma, those who thoroughly understand the principle that mind itself is buddha, even if they do not chant sutras with their mouths or practice the buddha way with their bodies, still lack nothing at all of buddha-dharma. Simply knowing that the buddha-dharma exists in the self from the beginning is the perfect accomplishment of the Way. Outside of this, you should not seek from other people, much less take the trouble to engage the Way in zazen."

As Dōgen Zenji said in *Genjōkōan*, "to study the buddha way is to study the self." Thus, to study ourselves is the buddha way. If we only understand this "mind is itself buddha," we don't need to chant sutras or study dharma from texts or with a teacher. Moreover, we don't need to take the trouble to practice zazen. Isn't it true?

Dōgen Zenji replied to this question:

These words are total nonsense. If it is as you said, how could anyone with cognition fail to understand when taught this principle? You should know that buddha-dharma is studied by truly giving up the view that discriminates between self and others.

This is the final important point in *Bendōwa*. In the question it is said, "Simply knowing that the buddha-dharma exists in the self from the beginning is the perfect accomplishment of the Way." So this question is based on the theory that the mind is itself buddha. Dōgen Zenji counterargued saying:

If just knowing that the self is itself buddha was attainment of the Way, Shakyamuni would not have taken the trouble in ancient times to give guidance.

What is the difference between the self in the expression "the self is itself buddha" and the self mentioned by Dōgen Zenji when he said that to study the buddha way is to study the self?

We take for granted that this "I" is the self. How did we grasp this being (body and mind) as "I" in the beginning? First of all, this being was born as a crying baby. The baby sees various faces of different people appear and disappear in front of its eyes. Parents teach that these are all faces of human beings. The baby creates an image and concept of a human being in its mind, and gradually it starts to grasp that the baby itself is one human being, as an abstract concept. They think of the being as one person out of numerous human beings and finally discriminate the self from others.

However, buddha-dharma is not such an abstract concept. The self in Dōgen Zenji's expression is the self that is actually living as a fresh being, that is, the self that is only the self, the self out of the self. This self experiences the various life experiences. This is the all out of all, the self that is one with the whole universe. This is the true self that is living right now, right here.

Does this self exist as a substantial entity? No, it is always changing. The actual self is not something fixed. Though we are living right now, this present time becomes past in a twinkling and disappears. And the "I" of the future does not exist, because it is always an instant later than the present. This present time is the point of nothingness that has no time; it is like a reflection on a mirror that disappears in one instant. This is true self. The true self is universal, all out of all, and yet it is the point of nothingness.

On the contrary, it is entirely off the mark to think that the self is one out of numerous human beings and to separate the self from others, on that basis saying that this self is buddha, and buddha-dharma is in the individual self.

In order to illustrate this more clearly, Dōgen Zenji introduces the story of the director monk Gensoku. This story is interesting and easy to understand, so I will relate it briefly.

Once there was a temple director whose name was Gensoku in the assembly of Zen Master Hōgen Mon'eki. One day Hōgen asked Gensoku, "You are a student. Why haven't you ever asked me about buddha-dharma?"

Gensoku replied, "Once when I was at Zen Master Seihō's place, I realized the peace and joy of buddha-dharma."

So he didn't require anything anymore. This story starts here. Gensoku said he completely grasped buddha-dharma when Seihō said, "The fire boy comes seeking fire."

The fire boy is the god of fire. Gensoku understood that the god of fire coming to get fire means the self is seeking after the self.

Unexpectedly Hōgen scolded him unsparingly: "I really know that you don't understand. If buddha-dharma was like that it would not have been transmitted up to today."

Gensoku swelled with anger and immediately left. After a while, he changed his mind and came back to Hōgen. He apologized for his rudeness and asked Hōgen, "What is the self of this student?"

Truly, at this time his egotistic pride as "one person out of all" was taken away. Then Hōgen said, "The fire boy comes seeking fire."

Hōgen's reply is exactly the same as Seihō's. Although he heard the same words, Gensoku really realized buddha-dharma this time. How did he realize the dharma? He clearly understood that

to comprehend "The self is itself buddha" cannot be called understanding buddha-dharma. If the comprehension that self is itself buddha was the buddha-dharma, Zen Master Hōgen would not have used that saying for guidance or made such an admonishment.

This is really true. For example, I said that the true self is the self that is only the self, all out of all, one with everything in the universe. But if you understand these words only as words through the intellect, the self is just an abstract concept. You understand the words, but you don't see the reality.

For example, many kindergarten kids today are precocious because they learn words from watching television. I once heard kids in a bus chattering, "Do you have a girlfriend? Have you ever kissed her?" They understand these words only as words. They don't have vigorous desire for the other sex. When they become teenagers and begin to feel the urge of sex, they don't need words; boys and girls communicate with each other with only their eyes.

Buddha-dharma is about the vivid self before conceptualization. When we express it with words, only words as concepts are transmitted. It is really difficult to transmit buddha-dharma as vivid reality. "The comprehension that self is itself buddha" is not enough. Just be the self that is itself buddha.

From the time you first meet a good teacher, just genuinely inquire about the manners and standards for practice, single-mindedly engage in the way of zazen, and do not keep your mind stuck on a single knowledge or half comprehension. The wondrous method of buddha-dharma is not without meaning.

Buddha-dharma should not be grasped as abstract concepts. It should be actual reality as wholehearted practice of the way of zazen.

QUESTION SEVENTEEN:

We hear that through the ages in India and China, someone was enlightened to the Way by hearing the sound of bamboo, and another clarified the heart on seeing the color of blossoms. Needless to say, Great Teacher Shakyamuni Buddha certified the Way upon seeing the morning star, and Venerable Ananda clarified the dharma when the banner pole [signalling dharma meetings] toppled. Not only that, but among the Five Houses after the Sixth Ancestor many people clarified the mind ground with a single word or half phrase. Were they definitely only people who had engaged the way of zazen?

The person who was enlightened by hearing the sound of bamboo was Kyōgen Chikan; the one who clarified the mind ground on seeing the color of blossoms was Reiun Shigon. Shakyamuni attained enlightenment by seeing the bright star. Ananda clarified dharma when he was admonished to bring down the banner pole, which was the sign for having dharma battle, meaning throw down his ego. There were many other people who were enlightened by a single phrase. Not all of them practiced zazen, did they?

Dōgen Zenji replied that those people had no doubts at all about practice of the way of zazen. "They had no secondary person" means there is no separation between the person who sees and things to be seen, the person hearing and sounds to be heard, and the person who is enlightened and enlightenment. Only the reality of life is there.

QUESTION EIGHTEEN:

In the Western Heaven [India] and in China, people are inherently straightforward. On account of its being the Central Flower [of civilization, i.e., China], when buddha-dharma was expounded they understood very quickly. In our country, from ancient times people have lacked benevolence and wisdom, so shouldn't we regret that, because of being barbarians, it is difficult for us to grow the true seed? Also, home-leaving monks in this country are inferior even to laypeople of those great countries. Everybody here is stupid and narrow-minded. They deeply cling to artificial merits and admire superficial virtues. Even if such people do zazen, how could they actually achieve buddha-dharma?

I don't think I have to explain this question. This is a weak point for Japanese people since ancient times. People cling to artificial merits and admire superficial virtues. People like to do things that can succeed and gain some apparent reward. Is it okay for such people to practice zazen? Dōgen Zenji replied by saying that the Japanese people are not civilized, but

actualizing and entering buddha-dharma or sailing beyond delusion does not necessarily depend on the intelligence of the human and heavenly realms.

Since buddha-dharma is the reality of life, it has nothing to do with worldly conditions.

When I wanted to become a monk, I thought the situation of Japanese Buddhism was terribly degenerate. Also there are quite a few priests who deplore the decadence of Buddhism in Japan. But this situation does not matter. The point is whether we, ourselves, actually practice or not.

There must have been many foolish people in India even at the time of Shakyamuni. Dōgen Zenji introduces some examples:

Even when the Buddha was in this world, someone attained the fourth stage [of arhat] because of [being hit by] a handball.

There was a senile monk who couldn't comprehend the Buddha's teachings. He asked a young monk how he could get enlightened. The mischievous young monk made fun of him and said, "I'll teach you if you give me a feast." The old monk treated him, and after he had eaten the young monk brought out a handball. He threw the ball at the old monk's head and said, "You have attained the first stage." He struck the old monk's head with the ball again and said, "Now you have attained the second stage." At the third hit he said, "You have attained the third stage." At the fourth strike he said, "You have attained the final stage." When the senile monk was hit like this, he really attained arhathood and his face changed. The mischievous young monk made a prostration to him.

Another realized the great way through putting on an okesa.

There was a courtesan who once at a drinking bout danced like a clown while wearing an okesa. She was reborn in hell because of her ungodly deed. But in the next life, because of the merit of wearing the okesa, she became a nun disciple of Shakyamuni and attained arhathood. Her name was Rengeshiki (Utpalavarna in Sanskrit).

Seeing a senile old monk sitting silently, a woman with deep faith who had offered him a meal thereby opened up satori.

An aged monk who had just been ordained went out for takuhatsu, and an old lady offered him a meal. The uninformed old monk received and ate the food thankfully. After the meal, the donor asked the monk to give a dharma talk, but since he didn't know what to say he kept sitting silently in embarrassment. A little later while she was waiting for his preaching, the old lady fell asleep. The old monk tried to escape; he sneaked out of the house and ran. When the old lady woke up, she ran after him. When she caught the old monk, she made a prostration and apologized for having fallen asleep during his speech. The old monk also made a prostration and asked her pardon. At this time, both of them were enlightened.

There are many such interesting stories in Buddhist sutras. If we practice with true faith, to be intelligent or not does not matter.

All people are abundantly endowed with the true seeds of prajna.

Each and every one of us is living out the reality of life.

The foregoing mutual exchange of questions and answers between guest and host has been disordered and may be confusing. How many flowers have been created in the flowerless sky?

The eighteen questions and answers are as above. Dōgen Zenji said this talk is not reality, but is like illusory flowers in the sky.

However, the essential meaning of engaging the way of zazen has not yet been transmitted in this country, so people who aspire to know it must be sorrowful. For this reason, I have compiled some of what I saw and heard in foreign lands, and have written and preserved my brilliant teacher's true essence in order to make it heard by aspiring practitioners. Besides this, I don't have a chance now to also present the standards for monasteries or the regulations for temples, especially as they should not be treated carelessly.

Later Dōgen Zenji wrote *Eihei shingi* (Pure standards for the Zen community) in order to compile standards for monastic life.

Indeed, although our country is located to the east of the Dragon Ocean, far away through the clouds and mist, since the time of the Emperors Kinmei and Yōmei the buddha-dharma from the West has moved east, much to everyone's happiness. And yet philosophical categories and religious activities are overgrown and entangled, so that people are unhealthy in their practice. [Instead of that,] now by using ragged robes and old, repaired bowls till the end of this life, tying together a thatched hut by the blue cliffs and white rocks, and practicing upright sitting, the matter going beyond buddha will be instantly manifested, and the great matter of the study of one lifetime will be immediately fulfilled. This is precisely the admonition of Ryūge and the style passed on at Kukkutupada.

Buddhism was transmitted from India to China and from China to Japan. But in Japan Buddhist priests were caught up in philosophical arguments or complicated rituals

and ceremonies. The most essential, genuine practice was
not yet transmitted.

The situation has not yet changed much, even today.
Actually, wearing tattered robes and eating from broken
bowls, living in a hermitage in the mountains, and practicing
genuine zazen, is enough. In doing so, "the great matter of
the study of one lifetime will be immediately fulfilled."

Ryūge Koton was a disciple of Tōzan Ryokai. He made
the following verse:

> *Eating nuts from trees, wearing clothes made out of grass,*
> *mind is like the moon,*
> *no mind and no boundary.*
> *If someone asked where am I living,*
> *green water and blue mountains are my house.*

This is Ryūge's expression of his practice style.

The manner of this zazen should accord with the
Fukanzazengi, *which I formulated in the Karoku Period*
(1225–1227).

Dōgen Zenji wrote *Fukanzazengi* in 1227 while he was
staying at Kenninji, right after he returned from China.
Bendōwa and *Fukanzazengi* are a complementary pair of early
writings from before he established his own monastery.

Furthermore, although the spread of buddha-dharma
throughout the country should await the emperor's approval, if we
consider again the request [of Shakyamuni] at Vulture Peak, then
emperors, nobles, ministers, and generals now appearing in a
thousand trillion lands have all gratefully received Buddha's
approval and have come to be born because they did not forget
their dedication, through many lifetimes, to protect buddha-
dharma. Which of the regions where their control has extended is
not a buddha land?

Consequently, in circulating the way of the buddhas and
ancestors, we should not necessarily be selective about places or wait
upon conditions. Only do not think that today is the beginning [of
our spreading the dharma].

When Dōgen Zenji wrote *Bendōwa*, he had not yet

received permission from the government to spread the dharma and establish his own school. In the *Ninnōgokoku Hannyakyō* (Perfection of wisdom sutra for the guardian king's protection of the nation) it is said that Shakyamuni asked emperors, kings, generals, and ministers to protect buddha-dharma, and those people have been protecting the dharma since then up to the present. There are no lands that are not buddha's land. Therefore, Dōgen Zenji said he didn't need to wait for permission, or to be selective about places and conditions.

Afterword

I gave talks on *Bendōwa* at "Meetings to Taste the Meaning of Shōbōgenzō" held at Sōsenji in Kyoto each month from November 1978 to July 1979. This book was transcribed and edited [in Japanese] by Ishiguro Kenichi from the record of my talks.

At the same time, I was working on another book *Jinseika Dokuhon* (Text on human life). Because of it I was so busy that publication of this book was delayed. But I am grateful that, through this work, I could deepen myself.

Many records of *teishō*, commentaries, or translations of *Shōbōgenzō* into modern Japanese have been published. However, probably because people venerate the original text too much, it seems to me that they only put Dōgen Zenji's words into other Buddhist terminology.

My late teacher Sawaki Kōdō Roshi used to say that when we read Buddhist scriptures, we should illuminate our own mind with the ancient teachings and squeeze out the buddha-dharma as our own expression. I have been following my teacher's admonition and trying to appreciate *Shōbōgenzō* from a deeper perspective. I think this is the work of my closing years.

I am happy if readers follow *Shōbōgenzō* with me as their own matter, and appreciate it on the ground of their own lives.

Uchiyama Kōshō

The Translators

SHOHAKU OKUMURA is a priest and dharma successor of
Kōshō Uchiyama Roshi. He has practiced at Antaiji and
Zuioji in Japan; the Pioneer Valley Zendo in Massachusetts;
and the Kyoto Sōtō Zen Center. His six previously published
books of translations are *Dōgen's Pure Standards for the Zen
Community: A Translation of "Eihei Shingi"*; *Opening the Hand
of Thought*; *Shikan Taza: An Introduction to Zazen*; "*Shōbōgenzō
Zuimonki*": *Sayings of Eihei Dōgen Zenji*; *Dōgen Zen*; and *Zen
Teaching of "Homeless" Kōdō*. Okumura Sensei, formerly head
teacher at the Minnesota Zen Meditation Center, is currently the Director of the North American Sōtō School in
Los Angeles.

TAIGEN DAN LEIGHTON is a priest in the lineage of Shunryu
Suzuki Roshi. He has practiced at the New York and San
Francisco Zen Centers, was head monk at Tassajara Zen
Mountain Center, and practiced for two years in Japan. He is
co-translator of *Cultivating the Empty Field: The Silent
Illumination of Zen Master Hongzhi*; *Dōgen's Pure Standards for
the Zen Community: A Translation of "Eihei Shingi"*; and *Moon
in a Dewdrop: Writings of Zen Master Dōgen*; and is author of
the forthcoming *Bodhisattva Archetypes: Classic Buddhist Guides
to Awakening and Their Modern Expression*. Leighton currently
teaches at the Green Gulch Farm Zen Center in Muir Beach,
California, and at the Institute of Buddhist Studies of the
Berkeley Graduate Theological Union.